T0383454

FRENCH BOULANGERIE

FERRANDI Paris

Project Coordinator: Audrey Janet
Chefs: Didier Chaput and Arnaud Savina
Students: Sum Yee Leung, Ravisankar Venus,
Vassileios Xanthopoulos, Lauren Zahn, and the students
of the CAP Connexe Boulanger program

Flammarion

French Edition
Editor: Clélia Ozier-Lafontaine, assisted by Laurie Perbost
Editorial Collaboration: Estérelle Payany
Design: Alice Leroy

English Edition
Editorial Director: Kate Mascaro
Editor: Helen Adedotun
Translation from the French: Ansley Evans
Copyediting: Wendy Sweetser
Typesetting: Alice Leroy
Proofreading: Nicole Foster
Indexing: Chris Bell

Production: Marylou Deserson and Louisa Hanifi
Color Separation: IGS-CP, L'Isle d'Espagnac

Printed in China by Toppan Leefung

Simultaneously published in French as
Boulangerie, Viennoiserie: Recettes et Techniques
d'une École d'Excellence

editions.flammarion.com
@flammarioninternational

23 24 25 3 2 1
ISBN: 978-2-08-043333-6
Legal Deposit: 11/2023

FERRANDI
PARIS

FRENCH BOULANGERIE

RECIPES AND TECHNIQUES FROM THE FERRANDI SCHOOL OF CULINARY ARTS

Photography by Rina Nurra

Flammarion

PREFACE

For over one hundred years, **FERRANDI Paris** has taught all of the culinary disciplines to students from around the world. Following the success of our five previous works published by Flammarion—a comprehensive guide to the art of French patisserie, as well as volumes focused on cooking with chocolate, vegetables, fruit and nuts, and charcuterie—it is now time to delve into the world of breads and *viennoiserie*, whose immense diversity requires both inventiveness and technical skill on the part of the baker. Celebrated French loaves and pastries—from baguettes to *pain de campagne*, or from croissants to brioches—all form part of the French culinary heritage that our teachers are committed to keeping alive. The chefs at **FERRANDI Paris** are continually enriching this repertoire with regional recipes from around France (such as kougelhopfs and fougasses) and the world (pita, panettone, babka, and more).

Both traditional skills and creative innovation lie at the heart of **FERRANDI Paris**'s teaching philosophy. We maintain a balance between the two through strong ties to the professional world, making our school the leading institution that it is today. That is why this book not only provides delicious recipes, but also demonstrates fundamental techniques and shares expert advice. Anyone who wishes to explore the inspiring world of breads and *viennoiserie*, whether it be at home or in a professional kitchen, will find this volume an invaluable reference.

I extend my warmest thanks to the members of **FERRANDI Paris** who have brought this book to fruition, particularly Audrey Janet, who coordinated the project, and Didier Chaput and Arnaud Savina, chef instructors at the school, who have generously shared their expertise and adeptly combined technical skills and imagination to demonstrate the culinary richness of the art of the French boulangerie.

Richard Ginioux
Executive Director of FERRANDI Paris

CONTENTS

INTRODUCTION

A Portrait of
FERRANDI Paris

In over one hundred years of history, **FERRANDI Paris** has earned an international reputation as one of the premier culinary and hospitality schools in France. Since its inception, the school—hailed "the Harvard of gastronomy" by the press—has trained generations of leading chefs and hospitality professionals. Whether at its historic campus in the Saint-Germain-des-Prés district in Paris, or its campuses in Saint-Gratien, Bordeaux, Rennes, or Dijon, **FERRANDI Paris** is dedicated to world-class teaching with the aim of training future leaders in hotel and restaurant management, hospitality entrepreneurship, and the culinary arts, including pastry and bread making.

Founded more than a century ago by the Paris Île-de-France Regional Chamber of Commerce and Industry, **FERRANDI Paris** is the only school in France to offer a full range of degree and certification programs in the culinary and hospitality arts, from vocational training to the master's degree level, in addition to international programs. The school takes pride in its 98 percent exam pass rate, which is the highest in France for degrees and certifications in the sector. No matter the level, a **FERRANDI Paris** education is rigorous and combines a mastery of the basics with an emphasis on innovation, management and entrepreneurial skills, and hands-on practice in a professional environment.

Strong Ties to the Professional World

A space for discovery, inspiration, and exchange—where the culinary arts mingle with science, technology, and innovation—**FERRANDI Paris** brings together the most prestigious and innovative names in the hospitality sector and creative culinary world. The school trains 2,200 apprentices and students each year, in addition to three hundred international students of over thirty nationalities and two thousand adults who come to the school to perfect their skills or change careers. The one hundred instructors at the school are all highly qualified: several have received prominent culinary awards and distinctions, such as the Meilleur Ouvrier de France (Best Craftsman in France) title, and all have at least ten years of work experience in the culinary field in prestigious establishments in France and abroad. To give students maximum opportunities and the chance to connect with other fields and the greater global community, the school has formed collaborative partnerships with several other institutions. In France, partner schools include the ESCP Europe Business School and AgroParisTech; abroad, the school collaborates with Johnson and Wales University in the United States, the ITHQ tourism and hotel management school in Canada, Hong Kong Polytechnic University, Macao Institute for Tourism Studies, and Başkent University in Turkey, among others. Since theory and practice go hand in hand, and because **FERRANDI Paris** strives for excellence in teaching, students also have the chance to participate in a number of official events through partnerships with several chief culinary associations in France, including Maîtres

Cuisiniers de France, Société des Meilleurs Ouvriers de France, Euro-Toques, and more. In addition, the school offers numerous prestigious professional competitions and prizes, giving students many opportunities to demonstrate their skills and knowledge. A dedicated ambassador of French culture, **FERRANDI Paris** draws students from around the world every year and is a member of the French Interministerial Tourism Council; the Collège Culinaire de France (an association dedicated to upholding culinary craftsmanship); the Strategic Committee of Atout France (the French tourism development agency); and the Conférence des Formations d'Excellence au Tourisme (CFET), a group of institutions in France offering top-quality training in tourism-related fields.

Extensive Savoir Faire

FERRANDI Paris's expertise, combining practice and close collaboration with professionals in the field, has been shared in five previous volumes devoted to French patisserie (which received a Gourmand World Cookbook award), chocolate making, vegetables, fruits and nuts, and charcuterie, intended for both professional chefs and amateur cooks alike. In this next book in the successful series, **FERRANDI Paris** now brings the art of the French boulangerie into the spotlight, focusing on breads and *viennoiseries*. From French classics, such as baguettes, country and whole wheat boules, fougasses, brioches, and *pain de mie*, to modern or international recipes including pretzels, panettone, babka, and cruffins, this book offers a world tour of bread-making expertise.

Breads, *viennoiseries*, and other delicacies

Long a symbol of sharing, bread nourishes both the body and mind. At its most basic level, bread is a combination of flour, water, levain or yeast, and a little salt, yet it also involves time and controlled fermentation. Above all, bread is a product of knowledge perfected over millennia that varies from country to country. The fact that so many recipes have evolved from these few simple ingredients reflects the skill and creativity of generations of bakers who have shared and passed on their craft. Made from wheat, rye, spelt, and a whole host of other grains, breads are incredibly diverse. Enriched with milk, butter, and eggs—and made with unique techniques including laminating, which results in buttery, flaky layers—*viennoiseries* are equally impressive. Whether enjoyed for breakfast or as a teatime snack, treats such as brioches, croissants, cinnamon rolls, and *kouign-amann* are always a delight to eat. In this book, **FERRANDI Paris** professionals explore the infinite range of fermentations, shapes, techniques, and recipes for breads and *viennoiseries* from France and around the world, for all to savor. Time to get kneading!

FRENCH BOULANGERIE: THE ESSENTIALS

Although the exact origins of bread making have been lost in time, it is certain that humans have made loaves combining the same basic ingredients for millennia: flour, water, salt, and the magic of fermentation. However, methods have evolved over the years, fine-tuned by generations of bakers worldwide. In this book, **FERRANDI Paris** professionals share their expertise through techniques and recipes that celebrate the renowned art of the French boulangerie. This introduction offers an overview of the main ingredients and stages in bread making, in addition to a few basic definitions, to help you succeed in making the recipes that follow.

Ingredients

Flour

Flour is the main ingredient in bread. Without a modifier, the term almost always refers to wheat flour, but it has been extended to encompass the fine powders produced by grinding different seeds and grains. Naturally rich in gluten, common wheat (*Triticum aestivum*)—also known as bread wheat—is the most frequently used grain in bread making. It is also among the most widely produced cereal crops in the world.

Wheat kernels consist of an outer layer made of cellulose (known as the "bran"), an endosperm containing the starch and proteins, and a germ that is rich in oil. Depending on how a given flour is milled, it will be more or less whole grain (whole wheat or wholemeal). French flours are categorized on a scale ranging from T150 (100 percent whole grain) to T45 (the whitest), with the letter "T" representing the mineral (or ash) content per 100 g (3.5 oz.) of flour. The whiter the flour (i.e., the more refined it is), the less bran, or minerals, it contains: from 0.45 percent in T45 flour to 1.5 percent in T150 flour. Individual flours within each "T" category present different bread-making qualities, depending on their "strength": the amount of protein (especially gluten) they contain.

Stoneground flour is obtained by grinding grains between two millstones, rather than metal cylinders. This method retains the germ and some of the bran, which makes the flour more nutritious.

There are six categories of French flour. Although American and British flours differ in mineral and protein content, the following chart suggests near equivalents. The original French flours used in the recipes in this book have been left in parentheses in the ingredients lists for bakers who wish to source them. Some bakers also combine different flours to mimic the French flour types.

French flour types

Type	Other names in French	Nearest US/UK equivalents	Typical uses
T45	*Farine blanche, farine de gruau*	Cake and pastry flour, or all-purpose flour	*Viennoiseries*, pastries, pizzas
T55	*Farine blanche, farine de gruau*	All-purpose flour	Standard white breads, puff pastries
T65	*Farine blanche*	White bread flour	White breads
T80	*Farine bise*	White whole wheat flour	Country breads
T110	*Farine semi-complète*	Light whole wheat flour	Whole wheat breads
T150	*Farine complète*	Dark/100% whole wheat flour	Bran breads

Other flours

Name	Characteristics	Description
Rye flour	Low in gluten but suitable for bread making. Deeply flavorful and mildly acidic. Often used to start a *levain-chef*.	Rye contains mucilage, which makes leavening more difficult to master; this is why rye flour is often mixed with an equal amount of white wheat flour.
Buckwheat flour	Gluten free. Grayish in color with a slightly bitter taste. Oxidizes quickly.	Despite its name, buckwheat is not actually wheat. It is used to make Breton crêpes because it has no rising power, and can be combined with other gluten-free grains to make gluten-free bread.
Einkorn flour	Low in gluten but suitable for bread making. Slightly yellow with a mild hazelnut flavor. Turns rancid easily.	A cousin of common wheat, low-yielding einkorn (*Triticum monocuccum*) is making a comeback due to its high nutritional value. It produces dense loaves that do not rise much but are nutritionally rich.
Spelt flour	Suitable for bread making. Mild nutty flavor.	A cold-weather grain, *Triticum spelta* is hardier and richer in fiber than wheat and must be husked before grinding. Doughs using spelt flour need less water and maintain their shape well during baking.
Corn flour	Gluten free. Bright yellow or white, depending on the type of corn used. Slightly sweet, intense flavor.	As it is gluten free, corn flour is best used in combination with other flours. Be sure not to confuse it with cornstarch, which has very different properties.
Rice flour	Gluten free. Very neutral in flavor. Gives a crumbly, sandy texture.	Made from brown or white rice, rice flour is particularly fine. It should not be confused with rice starch or the coarser "cream of rice."
Chestnut flour	Gluten free. Mild and sweet; remarkably fragrant.	Milled from dried roasted chestnuts, chestnut flour is rich in protein and fiber and is naturally gluten free, so it is not suitable on its own for bread making. It is mainly used for crêpes, tea cakes, etc.

Gluten and strength

Discovered in 1745, gluten is formed when two proteins (gliadin and glutenin) contained in certain grains—including wheat, barley, and rye—come into contact with water during the kneading process. The name *gluten*, which means *glue* in Latin, alludes to the protein's role: it gives dough elasticity and viscosity, and traps the CO_2 released during fermentation. It helps produce loftier, lighter loaves with a pleasantly chewy texture. Wheat flour contains 8–15 percent gluten: the more it contains, the "stronger" it is, meaning it is more resistant to the deformations produced by levain and yeast. Measured using a special device, flour strength ranges from 100 to 300 W (the unit of measure, which is, unfortunately, rarely listed on commercial packaging).

Protein content	Recommended uses
8–10%	Pastries, puff pastry, sauces, crêpes, etc.
10–12%	Breads
12–15%	*Viennoiseries* (yeasted puff pastries)

In general, whiter flours are stronger than whole-grain flours, which are rich in bran and fiber.

Celiac disease is a chronic, intestinal autoimmune disorder linked to the ingestion of gluten, and sufferers must avoid any product containing even minute traces. Gluten intolerance is a sensitivity to gluten and not an autoimmune disorder, but it can cause similar symptoms; however, its effects on sufferers' health are usually short term, unlike celiac disease.

Levain

The starting point for bread making, levain is a mixture of flour and water that undergoes a natural fermentation process and makes doughs rise. Levain contains lactic acid bacteria and wild yeasts, naturally present in the flour. These microorganisms play a key role in the texture and flavor of bread, and also influence its keeping potential. In breaking down the carbohydrates in the flour, yeasts release CO_2, enabling dough to rise, while bacteria provide the acidity characteristic of levain-based breads. In accordance with French tradition, this book refers to a culture of fermented flour and water as levain, as opposed to a sourdough starter, although bakers often use the terms interchangeably.

It takes several days to make a levain that is ready for bread making. It can be made with a piece of dough taken from a previous batch of levain-based bread, or a *levain-chef* can be started from scratch (see technique p. 36). The *levain-chef* is ready to use when it rises and falls predictably

after each feeding and emits a beer-like smell: evidence of fermentation. A new *levain-chef* must be refreshed—fed with water and flour and left to ferment again—five or six times before it can be used to make bread (see techniques pp. 38 and 40). This process makes the fermentation time more consistent and refines the levain's flavors. Depending on the amount of water added, you obtain either a stiff levain (50 percent hydration, recommended for flavorful rustic breads with a thick crust), which has acetic aromas, or a liquid levain (100 percent hydration and milder in taste), with milky aromas. Once refreshed levain has reached peak fermentation, it is ready to be mixed into dough. At this point, it is considered "*tout point*": i.e., ripe and ready to leaven bread and maximize flavor.

Be sure to refresh your levain once it is expanded and bubbly (*tout point*), as waiting too long to feed it can affect the flavor of subsequent batches. A vigorous, healthy levain is remarkably resilient and can return to top form after a few regular feedings. If you only plan to bake once a week (or less), it is best to store your levain in the refrigerator, where it can hibernate for up to 2 weeks. After cold storage, levain will be sluggish and will need several feedings before it is *tout point* again. With regular attention, levain can live forever. Bakers pass theirs on from generation to generation, and some levains have famously been sold along with actual bakeries. Baking with levain is the oldest bread-making method, and although it fell out of favor in the 1920s, it has seen a revival in recent years

Commercial Yeast

Also known as baker's yeast, commercial yeast is industrially produced from a multitude of microscopic fungi of the *Saccharomyces cerevisiae* family. It comes fresh (also known as cake or compressed yeast) or dried (in granules, whether instant or active dry). Many recipes in this book call for fresh yeast, which can be found in the refrigerated sections of larger supermarkets, purchased online, or possibly sourced from your local bakery or pizzeria. If you cannot find it, substitute 50% of the weight of fresh yeast with active dry yeast, or 40% with instant yeast.

When combined with carbohydrates (contained in flour) and water, and placed in a warm environment—at least 75°F (24°C)—yeast cells proliferate, making dough rise faster and more reliably than levain-based doughs. *Viennoiseries* are typically made with commercial yeast, which can be used in pre-ferments (see below), or mixed directly with the other dough ingredients.

Pre-fermentation entails preparing a small amount of dough and leaving it to ferment for at least a few hours before kneading it into the main dough. This strengthens the gluten network and gives the flavor more time to develop. In addition to improving taste, pre-fermentation also strengthens weak flour and makes the final product last longer.

The main pre-fermentation methods used in this book are:

• *Pâte fermentée:* French for "fermented dough," *pâte fermentée* is simply a portion of dough reserved from a previous batch. It is a natural way to strengthen dough and boost flavor. It keeps for up to 3 days in the refrigerator (the flavor will be stronger the longer it ferments). If you do not have any leftover dough, you can prepare the *pâte fermentée* for a specific recipe the day before you make it: mix together ¾ cup + 2 tbsp (3.5 oz./100 g) flour, ¼ cup (60 g/60 ml) water, 0.05 oz. (1 g) fresh yeast, and 0.1 oz. (2 g) fine salt, scaling the quantities up or down as needed. Place in a clean bowl, cover, and refrigerate overnight (or up to 3 days) before using.

• Poolish (see technique p. 42): Made from flour, water, yeast, and sometimes salt, this highly fluid mixture ferments slowly to develop flavor and subtle acidity. It works well in recipes such as croissants or baguettes. Poolish must be used as soon as it is ripe and cannot be stored.

Water

Just as important as flour, water binds all the dough ingredients together, and allows the magic of gluten formation and fermentation to take place. The quantity needed for each recipe depends on the type of flour used and the hydration level of the dough. It is best to use filtered water, or to allow the chlorine, which is volatile, to dissipate by letting the water stand for 12 hours before use. It should be noted that water temperature is the easiest parameter to control for optimal fermentation (see Desired dough temperature p. 20).

Salt

Beyond enhancing flavor, salt plays other key roles in bread making. It improves gluten strength by promoting protein binding, makes doughs firm by limiting water evaporation, improves flavor development by lengthening the fermentation time, produces a more uniform crumb, and favors the formation of a thin, nicely colored crust. Lastly, it also improves the keeping quality of bread once baked. On the flip side, salt inhibits the development of microorganisms, so avoid putting it in direct contact with levain or yeast since it can slow or even halt the fermentation process.

For *viennoiserie*

Sugar

Sugars do far more than just sweeten dough. Superfine, granulated, powdered, and brown sugars—as well as other sweeteners like honey—enhance *viennoiserie* in many ways. In addition to boosting the fermentation process by feeding the yeasts, they also make the crumb more tender and moist, encourage the crust to brown more quickly, and—by retaining water—improve the storage time of baked goods.

Milk

Milk is the liquid of choice in many *viennoiserie* recipes, replacing water partially or entirely. This makes dough soft and moist and helps it to brown more quickly in the oven. References to milk in these recipes are always to cow's milk, and if the type is not specified, you can choose from whole or low-fat milk. Use fresh pasteurized or UHT milk, not raw milk.

Butter

Unless the ingredients for a recipe state otherwise, use unsalted butter, preferably with a fat content of at least 82%. The higher its fat content, the less water the butter contains, which equates to flakier crusts. A high butterfat content is particularly important when making laminated doughs such as puff pastries, which benefit from butter with a minimum of 84% fat. When a recipe calls for softened or room temperature butter, remove it from the refrigerator at least 30 minutes before starting.

Eggs

The eggs used in these recipes are hen's eggs. As precision is crucial in bread and *viennoiserie* making, most egg quantities are given by weight and volume, in addition to an approximate number of eggs. This number is based on a standard "large" egg in the US and Canada and a "medium" egg in the UK, with an average in-shell weight of about 2 oz. (55 g).

Measuring ingredients

For successful results, it is always advisable to weigh your ingredients—including liquids—using a digital scale and preferably using metric weights. The volume and imperial measures included throughout this book have been rounded up or down to avoid awkward or unmeasurable amounts. When using cups and spoons, they must be level unless stated otherwise.

Baker's percentage or baker's math

If you wish to scale a recipe up or down, the baker's percentage comes in handy. However, it only applies to metric measures. In this dough formula, the total weight of the flour represents 100 percent, and all the other ingredients are expressed as a percentage of the flour weight. To determine the percentage of the other ingredients, divide the weight of each by the flour weight in grams, then multiply the result by 100. For example, if a recipe contains 500 g flour and 350 g water, the formula would be (350 ÷ 500) × 100 = 70%. If you want to scale the recipe up and use 750 g flour, you'd need 70% of this weight in water (525 g), and so on for the other ingredients.

The stages of bread making

Once levain has been refreshed and reached peak fermentation (*tout point* or ripe), it is time to make bread. Each step is important to ensure successful results.

Kneading

Whether using a stand mixer or your hands, the bread-making process begins by mixing the ingredients together. This hydrates the flour, incorporates air, and starts developing the gluten network, which will eventually trap the CO_2 produced by the yeast or levain. The temperature of the water used influences the dough temperature and is a particularly important parameter for optimal fermentation (see Desired dough temperature, right). The kneading stage starts by combining all the dough ingredients until they come together: this slow-speed mixing process, known as *frasage* in French, typically lasts for 3–5 minutes. In some cases, the flour and water in a recipe are combined first and left to rest for 30 minutes–1 hour before adding the remaining ingredients. This optional step, called autolyse, hydrates the flour and relaxes the gluten network, which makes the dough more extensible and reduces the kneading time, which is of particular interest for long-fermented breads. Next comes the rapid kneading phase, which gives the dough structure by developing the gluten network further and incorporating air. The dough texture can be adjusted by adding a small amount of liquid (***bassinage***) or flour (***contre-frasage***) at the end of the kneading stage. The desired dough consistency depends on the type of bread you are making: soft dough, which requires two fermentation stages, produces an open crumb; *bâtard* dough has more body and produces different-sized holes in the crumb; and stiff dough results in a tight crumb.

To ensure the dough is sufficiently kneaded, perform the windowpane test: stretch out a small piece of dough between your hands. If it stretches until thin and transparent without tearing, it is ready. Aim for this level of development when kneading dough for *viennoiserie* and pizzas. For slow-rising, levain-based doughs, this will occur at the end of the bulk fermentation process, after several sets of folds (see technique p. 48). This test is not suitable for doughs using whole wheat flour with bran or doughs that include seeds, chopped nuts, etc.

Desired dough temperature (DDT)

The dough temperature significantly influences the rate of fermentation, so it plays a crucial role in leavening and flavor. For optimal results, the dough temperature should be 73°F–79°F (23°C–26°C) after kneading. This is especially important for professional bakers, who need to maintain consistency loaf after loaf. To obtain the DDT, professionals use a formula to calculate the variable that is easiest to adjust: water temperature. The formula also takes room temperature, flour temperature, and friction factor (the heat generated by the kneading method) into consideration. To determine the ideal water temperature, multiply the DDT by 3 (or by 4 if using levain or a preferment). Then subtract the temperatures of the flour, room, friction factor, and levain, if using. Figure a friction factor of 0°F (0°C) for hand kneading and around 25°F or 18°C (different scales used for °F and °C) for a stand mixer.

Ideal water temp. = DDT × 3 (or 4 if using levain) – flour temp. – room temp. – 25°F or 18°C

Home bakers need not be so concerned with these calculations; just bear in mind that if the room temperature is warm, cool (but not icy) water should be used, and, conversely, if it is cool, warm (but never hot) water should be used.

Fermentation

The fermentation process is generally divided into two phases: bulk fermentation (the first rise) and proofing (the second rise). This is when the levain and/or yeast come into play, consuming the sugars present in the flour and giving off byproducts such as alcoholic compounds, which influence dough flavor and strength, and CO_2, which makes the dough rise. Controlling the fermentation times and temperatures is essential to successful bread making.

Shaping

The shaping of the dough takes place after the bulk fermentation phase and is usually followed by a second fermentation phase: proofing. Some doughs must be **pre-shaped** and left to rest before giving them their final form. Shaping not only gives the dough a specific form, but also restores its strength after bulk fermentation. Whether shaping a boule, baguette, *bâtard*, *épi*, or bun, mastering the technique is a matter of practice.

Proofing

For doughs that require proofing, timing is key. Underproofed dough will not have enough gas to rise, while overproofed dough, with a weakened gluten network, may collapse during baking. Although the recipes provide proofing times, the exact time needed depends on many factors, including the proofing temperature. To ensure dough is sufficiently proofed and ready for the oven, you can do the **poke test**. Gently press your finger into the dough: if the dough springs back quickly, it is underproofed; if it does not spring back, it is overproofed. If the dough springs back slowly and a small indentation remains where it was poked, it is ready to bake.

Scoring

Some doughs must be scored—slashed with a decisive, quick movement, often using a bread lame—either after shaping or, more usually, after proofing, before going into the oven. Scoring is not only aesthetically pleasing, but it also maximizes **oven spring**. These strategic cuts allow the steam and CO_2 to escape during baking, helping the bread to expand while rising. Certain types of bread (including ciabatta, focaccia, sandwich bread, and low-gluten breads like rye or einkorn) do not need to be scored.

Baking and cooling

A crucial step in bread making, baking is tricky to master in a home kitchen due to the differences between domestic and professional ovens. Professional bakers use deck ovens with high thermal inertia. It is hard to obtain the same results in home ovens, in which you cannot bake directly on the oven floor. But with a little trial and error, it is possible to make bakery-worthy bread at home. The moment the dough goes into the oven is especially important. In a final burst of fermentation, the dough rapidly expands, producing what is known as **oven spring**. To maximize this process, the oven must be fully preheated to the desired temperature. Professional bakers also add an injection of steam, which not only keeps the dough surface moist, allowing it to expand easily, but also adds shine and encourages the crust to color evenly. Using a preheated bread stone, heavy-duty baking sheet, or Dutch oven (see technique p. 59) are other ways to achieve professional-looking results at home. After removing most breads and *viennoiseries* from the oven, it is best to let them cool on a rack before cutting (*ressuage*). This ensures a crisp crust and allows the flavors developed during fermentation and baking to meld.

How to bake with steam on a hot baking sheet or stone:

• Place a heavy-duty baking sheet or baking stone on a rack in the center of the oven (to recreate the conditions of a professional deck oven) and an empty heavy-duty rimmed baking sheet on the bottom rack. If using a baking stone, follow the manufacturer's recommended preheating times.

• Preheat the oven to the desired temperature and bring 1 cup (250 ml) water to a simmer.

• Place the proofed dough on a sheet of parchment paper or a flour-dusted peel to make it easier to transfer to the oven.

• Slide the dough (on the parchment paper, if using) onto the hot baking sheet or stone once the oven is fully preheated.

• Immediately pour the simmering water into the pan on the lower rack to create steam and quickly close the oven door. Be sure to wear oven mitts and protect yourself from the burst of hot steam.

Note: Thicker baking sheets and stones retain more heat and so produce better results. This encourages oven spring and makes the crust wonderfully crisp. Some breads require drying, to develop a thicker, crisper crust, which is why some recipes say to open the oven door toward the end of the baking time to release steam and then lower the oven temperature. This allows the bread to finish baking without browning the crust further.

Storing and freezing breads and *viennoiseries*

It is best to store moist, tender breads (such as sandwich bread, buns, and pita bread) in plastic bags or well covered with plastic wrap to keep them soft. Breads with crisp crusts keep better wrapped in a clean dish towel. Store dry breads, such as crackers or breadsticks (see recipe p. 196), in an airtight container, preferably made of metal. When a recipe produces a greater quantity than you need, freezing is a good solution for the surplus. For breads such as baguettes (see recipes pp. 128–33), parbaking is recommended. Bake the dough until the first signs of coloring, then remove the loaves from the oven and let them cool completely on a rack. Cover airtight with plastic wrap and freeze. To finish baking, preheat the oven according to the recipe and bake directly from the freezer, adding a burst of steam (see above), until done. The bread will be fresh and crisp. In contrast, it is best to bake *viennoiseries* completely before freezing them. After they have fully cooled, carefully cover them with plastic wrap, taking care not to crush the puff pastry layers, and freeze. To serve, defrost on a rack and warm in the oven at 300°F (150°C/Gas Mark 2) for 4–5 minutes.

Glossary of boulangerie terms

AUTOLYSE
A resting stage after the flour and water in a recipe have been mixed together, before adding the remaining dough ingredients (see technique p. 44).

BASSINAGE
The addition of a small percentage of the total water in a recipe at the end of the kneading stage, to adjust the dough texture.

BOULANGERIE
The French word for a bakery that sells mostly breads and *viennoiseries*. In France, the term can only be used for stores that make their own bread.

BULK FERMENTATION (*POINTAGE*)
The first resting period after kneading and the first stage in fermentation, also known as the **first rise**.

COOLING (*RESSUAGE*)
The essential stage just after the bread is removed from the oven: it is placed on a rack to allow steam trapped inside the loaf to gradually evaporate outward through the crust, optimizing flavor and texture.

ELASTICITY
The capacity of a dough to return to its original shape or spring back after it has been stretched.

LEVAIN
A natural culture derived from the spontaneous fermentation of water and flour used to leaven bread. It is also known as **sourdough starter**. The term ***levain-chef*** refers to the master (or mother) culture that is refreshed or fed to produce ***levain tout point*** (ripe levain), which has reached peak fermentation and is ready to be mixed into dough.

OVEN SPRING
The final burst of fermentation that occurs right after the dough goes into the oven, causing the dough to expand rapidly. The greater the oven spring, the airier the crumb.

PROOFING (*APPRÊT*)
The second resting period after shaping dough (also called the **second rise**) and the final fermentation stage before baking.

REFRESHING
Feeding levain with flour and water to keep it robust or get it ready for baking (see techniques pp. 38 and 40).

SEAM (*CLÉ*)
The place where two dough edges meet, created by shaping. Dough may be baked with the seam facing up or down, depending on the loaf.

SUPPLE
Used to describe a dough that is pliant with a certain degree of extensibility. Soft doughs may be supple but not necessarily elastic.

VIENNOISERIE
French baked goods leavened with yeast or levain and frequently enriched with milk, butter, eggs, and/or sugar. The doughs are often laminated. Generally less sweet than pâtisseries, *viennoiseries*—including croissants and brioches—are typically eaten for breakfast in France.

WATER DOUGH (*DÉTREMPE*)
Made with flour, water, and salt, water dough is the first step in puff pastry recipes before incorporating the laminated butter. In this book, it is referred to as **base dough** when made with milk instead of water.

EQUIPMENT

1. Baker's couche
2. Flour bench brush
3. Bread lame
4. Scissors
5. Dough docker
6. Bench scraper
7. Bowl scraper

1. Fine grater or zester
2. Rolling pin
3. Whisk
4. Pastry brush
5. Instant-read thermometer

1. Offset spatula
2. Palette knife
3. Large flexible spatula
4. Small flexible spatula
5. Firm spatula

1. Paring knife
2. Chef's knife
3. Serrated knife

1. Assorted cloth-lined bannetons (proofing baskets)
2. Assorted rattan bannetons (proofing baskets)
3. Glass canning jars
4. Bread peel
5. Baguette peel
6. Fluted apple turnover cutter
7. Star-shaped cookie cutters

1. Cooling rack
2. Kougelhopf mold
3. Brioche mold
4. Individual brioche molds
5. Pullman (*pain de mie*) loaf pan

1. Pastry bag
2. Assorted pastry tips

1. Stand mixer with attachments:
   A. Dough hook
   B. Whisk
   C. Paddle beater

TECHNIQUES

BREAD

Levain-Chef (Master Levain)

Makes 6.75 oz. (190 g)

Active time
5 minutes

Fermentation time
About 24–48 hours at room temperature, until ready to be refreshed (see "What Next?" p. 37)

Ingredients
¾ tsp (5 g) honey
Scant ½ cup (100 g/100 ml) water at 113°F (45°C)
¾ cup (3 oz./85 g) rye flour (or whole wheat flour)

Equipment
Whisk
Glass canning jar

1 • Place the honey and water in a large bowl and whisk to dissolve the honey.

CHEFS' NOTES

• The fermentation time depends on the flour used, the room temperature, the ambient humidity, and the season. This explains the large difference between the minimum and maximum fermentation times. The process will take longer in a cooler environment.

• Honey activates the fermentation process. You can omit the honey, although it will take longer for the cultures to become active.

2 • Whisk in the flour.

3 • Transfer the mixture to a clean jar, close the jar, and let ferment in a warm place (ideally at around 95°F/35°C). Fermentation will take longer in a cooler place.

4 • When the mixture begins to have a distinct odor, large bubbles appear, and the texture resembles chocolate mousse, it must be refreshed to keep the culture alive and make the levain robust enough for baking (see "What Next?").

WHAT NEXT?

The *levain-chef* cannot be used at this stage; it must be refreshed (or fed) 5 or 6 times before it is *tout point*, i.e., ripe and ready to be used in a recipe. If you require a stiff levain, follow the technique on p. 38; if you require a liquid levain, follow the technique on p. 40. It should take about a week of refreshing and fermentation to obtain a levain *tout point*.

Refreshing *Levain-Chef* to Make Stiff Levain

Makes 10.5 oz. (300 g) stiff levain

Active time

5 minutes

Fermentation time

5 hours or more, depending on the room temperature

Storage

Up to 24 hours at warm room temperature and several days in the refrigerator once established (after chilling, refresh it as needed until *tout point*—ripe and ready to use)

Ingredients

2 oz. (60 g) *levain-chef* (see technique p. 36)

⅓ cup (80 g/80 ml) water at 95°F (35°C)

Scant 1½ cups (5.5 oz./160 g) stoneground white whole wheat flour (T80)

Equipment

Stand mixer + dough hook

Glass canning jar large enough for the levain to double in volume

1 • Place the levain and water in the bowl of the stand mixer.

2 • Mix to loosen the levain and create small bubbles to activate the bacteria and yeast in the levain.

3 • Incorporate the flour and mix on low speed for 5 minutes.

CHEFS' NOTES

- A stiff *levain-chef* is considered "established" and ready to use when it consistently doubles in volume after each feeding.
- Stiff levain will have an acidic and slightly vinegary smell and taste.

4 • Turn the levain out onto a work surface. Knead it by folding the bottom and top edges inward and then flattening it.

5 • Rotate the dough 90° and fold the bottom and top edges inward.

6 • Roll between your hands on the work surface to form a taut, smooth ball. Store in a clean, heavy airtight jar (one able to withstand pressure) and keep in a warm place (ideally at around 82°F/28°C) for fermentation. If it is cooler, the process will take longer.

7 • The stiff levain is *tout point*, i.e., ripe and ready to use, when it has doubled in volume, begins to collapse slightly, and cracks appear on the surface. The levain is considered "young" right before it reaches its peak. Weigh out the amount you need for your recipe, refresh the rest, and store.

Refreshing *Levain-Chef* to Make Liquid Levain

Makes 10.5 oz. (300 g) levain

Active time

5 minutes

Fermentation time

5 hours or more, depending on the room temperature

Storage

Up to 24 hours at warm room temperature and several days in the refrigerator once established (after chilling, refresh it as needed until *tout point*—ripe and ready to use)

Ingredients

½ cup (120 g/120 ml) water at 113°F (45°C)

2 oz. (60 g) *levain-chef* (see technique p. 36)

1 cup (4 oz./ 120 g) white bread flour (T65)

Equipment

2 glass canning jars large enough for the levain to triple in volume

Flexible spatula

Whisk

1 • Pour the water over the levain in a jar or bowl. Using the spatula, stir to loosen.

2 • Pour the mixture into a large bowl and whisk until frothy to activate the microbes in the levain.

3 • Whisk in the flour.

4 • Pour into a clean jar and set aside in a warm place to ferment (ideally at around 95°F/35°C). The fermentation will take longer in a colder environment.

5 • The liquid levain is *tout point*, i.e., ripe and ready to use, when it has tripled in volume, large bubbles have formed on the surface, and cracks are just beginning to appear. The levain is considered "young" right before it reaches its peak. Weigh out the amount you need for your recipe, refresh the rest, and store.

CHEFS' NOTES

- A liquid *levain-chef* is considered "established" and ready to use when it consistently triples in volume after each feeding.
- Liquid levain will have a mild and slightly sweet and milky smell and taste, reminiscent of yogurt.

Poolish

Active time
5 minutes

Fermentation time
3 hours

Storage
Poolish must be used when it is ripe and cannot be stored

Equipment
Whisk
Clean glass jar

Ingredients
0.05 oz. (1 g) fresh yeast, crumbled
⅓ cup (80 g/80 ml) water
⅔ cup (3 oz./80 g) flour

1 • Whisk the yeast into the water in the mixing bowl until it has dissolved completely.

2 • Whisk in the flour until well combined.

3 • Transfer to the glass jar and close.

CHEFS' NOTES

To make poolish, you need equal amounts of flour and water.

The amount of fresh yeast depends on the fermentation time at room temperature, according to the following metric formula: **amount of water × 40 ÷ hours of fermentation**

For example:

4 cups (1 L) water	×	40	÷	1 hour fermentation	=	1.5 oz. (40 g) fresh yeast
4 cups (1 L) water	×	40	÷	10 hours fermentation	=	0.15 oz. (4 g) fresh yeast
2 cups (500 ml) water	×	40	÷	2 hours fermentation	=	0.35 oz. (10 g) fresh yeast
4 qt. (4 L) water	×	40	÷	8 hours fermentation	=	0.75 oz. (20 g) fresh yeast

4 • Let the poolish ferment for about 3 hours, until it has tripled in volume, it is just beginning to collapse, and cracks start to form on the surface. Use immediately.

Above: poolish before (left) and after (right) fermentation.

Autolyse

Active time
10 minutes

Resting time
At least 30 minutes (ideally several hours)

Equipment
Stand mixer + dough hook

Ingredients
Water
Flour
Fresh yeast
Salt

CHEFS' NOTES

The quantities of ingredients will depend on the recipe you are making. This technique is used in many bread recipes: it hydrates the flour completely, reduces kneading time, strengthens the dough, and boosts flavor.

1 • Place the water and flour in the bowl of the stand mixer. Mix for 3–5 minutes on low speed until no dry pockets of flour remain. The dough will not be elastic at this point and will tear when pulled.

2 • Let the dough rest for at least 30 minutes, or ideally for several hours, depending on the recipe. Cover the bowl with plastic wrap or a damp dish towel, ensuring it does not touch the dough. At the end of the autolyse process, the dough will be smoother and more extensible.

3 • Make two small wells in the dough. Crumble the yeast into one and add the salt to the other. Pull a little dough across the top of the wells so that the yeast and salt begin to dissolve.

Kneading Dough in a Stand Mixer

Ingredients

1½ cups (340 g/340 ml) water

4 cups + 2 tbsp
(1 lb. 2 oz./500 g) flour

0.25 oz. (5 g) fresh yeast

1¾ tsp (9 g) salt

Equipment

Stand mixer + dough hook

Instant-read thermometer

CHEFS' NOTES

To determine whether the dough has been sufficiently kneaded, touch it lightly with the back of your hand. If it sticks, it means the flour has not absorbed all the water and the dough needs additional kneading.

1 • Place the water and flour in the bowl of the stand mixer.

2 • Crumble in the yeast and add the salt. Knead on low speed for about 5 minutes, until the dough is smooth and no longer sticky. Continue kneading for an additional 5–8 minutes on high speed to develop the gluten network.

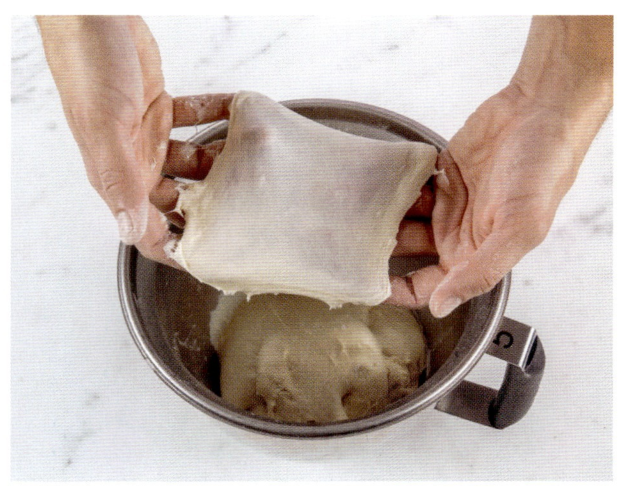

3 • At the end of the kneading process, the dough temperature should not exceed 75°F (24°C). To check for adequate gluten development, stretch a piece of dough until it is paper thin and light can be seen through it (windowpane test). If it does not tear, it is ready.

Kneading Dough by Hand

Ingredients
1½ cups (340 g/340 ml) water
1¾ tsp (9 g) salt
0.25 oz. (5 g) fresh yeast
4 cups + 2 tbsp (1 lb. 2 oz./500 g) flour

Equipment
Mixing bowl
Whisk
Bowl scraper
Instant-read thermometer

1 • Place the water and salt in the mixing bowl and crumble in the yeast. Whisk until the salt and yeast dissolve.

2 • Add the flour and mix it in using your fingertips until well combined. You can use the bowl scraper to help.

3 • Turn the dough out onto a floured work surface. Begin kneading by stretching the dough upward and outward.

4 • Fold the stretched dough over itself and knead again.

5 • Repeat stretching and folding the dough until it is supple and elastic. At the end of the kneading process, the dough temperature should not exceed 75°F (24°C). To check for adequate gluten development, stretch a piece of dough until it is paper thin and light can be seen through it (windowpane test). If it does not tear, it is ready.

Folding Dough

Ingredients
Bread or *viennoiserie* dough
Flour for dusting

1 • Place the dough on a floured work surface. Using your hands, deflate the dough and press it into a rectangle.

2 • Fold the bottom third of the dough up like a letter (the bottom part should now be the same size as the top part). Press down gently to seal the two parts together.

3 • Fold the top of the dough over to cover the bottom part.

4 • Check the strength of the dough by applying pressure with your fingertips. If the finger marks disappear, the dough is strong enough and does not need to be folded again (proceed to step 7).

5 • If the finger marks do not disappear, perform another fold: repeat steps 1–4, but work from the left to the right of the dough instead of top to bottom.

6 • Press down gently to seal the two parts together.

7 • Place the dough in a bowl lined with plastic wrap and cover until ready to use.

Shaping Dough into a Boule

Ingredients
Dough

CHEFS' NOTES

- The dough has sufficient strength if your fingertips do not leave a mark when pressed on the surface.
- To make a large boule, perform the same turning action using two hands: both little fingers should cup the dough at its base as you rotate it.

1 • Flatten the dough using the palm of your hand.

2 • Pull up one side of the dough to make a flap and fold this toward the center. The flap should be twice as long as the rest of the dough. Pull up a corner of the first fold and fold it toward the center. Continue around the dough. Make 7–8 folds for each boule, as the goal is to have as many as possible to give the dough strength.

3 • Turn the boule over and roll it against the work surface. Your thumb and little finger should touch the work surface and cup the dough gently at its base as you rotate it to make it smooth and taut.

Shaping Dough into a Baguette

Ingredients
Baguette dough (see recipes pp. 128–33)
Flour for dusting

1 • Place the baguette dough on a floured surface. Using the palm of your hand, flatten it to remove air bubbles and give it an elongated shape.

CHEFS' NOTES

You can use the same method to shape *ficelles* and *bâtards*.

• *Ficelles* are thin baguettes. Use half as much dough and make the shape twice as thin but the same length as a standard baguette.

• *Bâtards* are essentially short baguettes. Use the same quantity of dough but make the shape half as long as a standard baguette.

2 • Fold the top edge of the dough inward like a letter and press gently to seal. This folded part should be two-thirds of the width of the baguette.

Shaping Dough into a Baguette (continued)

3 • Flatten the dough well using the palm of your hand to remove any air bubbles.

4 • Fold the bottom edge of the dough inward like a letter and press down gently to seal. Flatten well again using the palm of your hand.

5 • Fold the dough in half to make a seam. Place your left thumb on the left end of the dough in the center to serve as a pivot. With your other hand, fold the dough over your thumb, pressing down gently on the seam of the fold to seal well. Continue in the same way working to the right end of the dough.

6 • Gently roll the dough against the work surface to make tapered ends.

Shaping Dough into an *Épi* (Wheat Stalk)

Ingredients

Dough with a short proofing time, shaped into baguettes (see technique p. 51) and proofed

Equipment

Scissors

CHEFS' NOTES

This shape is quite fragile and breaks easily, so take care when removing the baked loaf from the oven.

1 • At the end of the proofing time, when the dough is ready to bake, start near one end of a baguette and make a deep cut about three-quarters of the way into the dough at a 45-degree angle, using the scissors.

2 • Fold the cut piece out to the side like a kernel of wheat, keeping the scissors in place to prevent the dough from fusing back together. Repeat every 1½–2½ in. (4–6 cm), folding out the pieces on alternate sides, to obtain a complete wheat stalk.

Scoring Baguettes

Ingredients (for a 12-in./30-cm baguette)
Baguette dough (see recipes pp. 128 and 132), shaped (see technique p. 51) and proofed

Equipment
Bread lame

CHEFS' NOTES

The number of cuts depends on the length of the baguette:

4 in. (10 cm) and over	= 1 cut
8 in. (20 cm) and over	= 2 cuts
12 in. (30 cm) and over	= 3 cuts
16 in. (40 cm) and over	= 4 cuts
20 in. (50 cm) and over	= 5 cuts

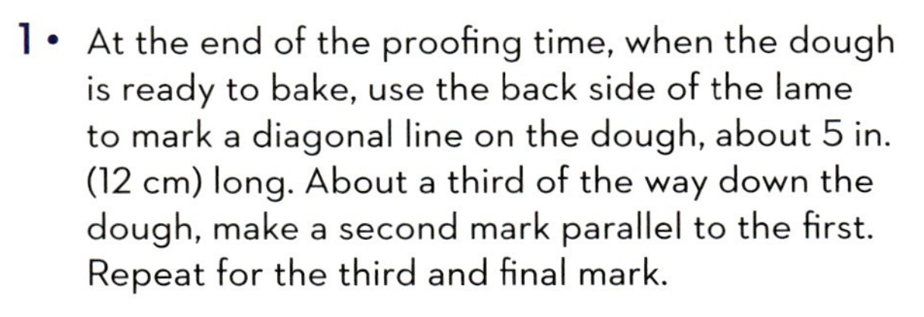

1 • At the end of the proofing time, when the dough is ready to bake, use the back side of the lame to mark a diagonal line on the dough, about 5 in. (12 cm) long. About a third of the way down the dough, make a second mark parallel to the first. Repeat for the third and final mark.

2 • Using the blade side, go over the marks you made in the first step. Keep the lame completely straight and cut about ¼ in. (5 mm) into the dough.

Scoring Boules

Ingredients

Dough shaped into boules (see technique p. 50) and proofed

Flour for dusting

Equipment

Bread lame

At the end of the proofing time, when the dough is ready to bake, dust the boules evenly with flour. Using the lame, make a straight cut across the center of each boule from one side to the other. Starting from the center, make perpendicular cuts on either side of this line to form a cross. Make diagonal slashes in each quarter.

CHEFS' NOTES

Make sure you never cut twice in the same place (in the center of the cross, for instance), because the dough will open up too much during baking.

Scoring Dough with a Chevron Cut

Ingredients

Dough that does not rise significantly, such as whole wheat, rye, or maslin, shaped

Flour for dusting

Equipment

Bread lame

After shaping the dough, dust it evenly with flour. Using the lame, make deep parallel cuts in the dough in a chevron pattern. Take care to leave about a finger's width of uncut space down the center of the dough.

Scoring Dough with Diagonal Slashes

Ingredients

Porous, fragile dough, such as rye or whole wheat, or dough for a Vienna-style bread, shaped

Flour for dusting

Equipment

Bread lame

After shaping the dough, dust it evenly with flour. Using the lame, make relatively deep parallel diagonal cuts across the dough at a 45-degree angle, making sure the cuts are evenly spaced.

CHEFS' NOTES

If the slashes are far apart, you can make them deeper so that the pattern stands out more after baking.

Scoring Dough with a Crosshatch (Polka) Cut

Ingredients

Porous, fragile, little-kneaded dough, principally levain, or doughs such as rye or whole wheat, shaped and proofed

Flour for dusting

Equipment

Bread lame

At the end of the proofing time, when the dough is ready to bake, dust it evenly with flour. Using the lame, make parallel diagonal cuts across the bread in one direction, then repeat in the opposite direction to obtain equal-sized diamonds.

CHEFS' NOTES

The deeper the cut, the flatter the bread will be after baking. Shallower cuts will produce a more rounded loaf.

Baking Bread in a Dutch Oven

Ingredients

About 2 lb. 4 oz. (1 kg) traditional or rustic sourdough baguette dough (see recipes p. 128 and p. 130, respectively), shaped into a boule or *bâtard*, depending on the shape of your Dutch oven, and proofed

Flour

Equipment

12 × 8-in. (30 × 20-cm) standard oval cast-iron or enamel Dutch oven

Cooking

45–50 minutes

CHEFS' NOTES

The Dutch oven evenly distributes heat and the lid traps steam inside, so it is not necessary to add any extra steam. It is an effective way to approximate the conditions of a professional oven in a domestic oven.

1 • Preheat the oven to 500°F (260°C/Gas Mark 10) with the covered Dutch oven inside.
Place the dough on a piece of parchment paper.
Dust it with flour and score it as you wish.

2 • Carefully remove the hot Dutch oven, lift off the lid using oven mitts, and place the dough inside, still on the parchment paper. Put the lid back on and place in the oven, without adding steam. Bake for 30 minutes.

3 • Remove the lid and continue to bake for 15–20 minutes, or until the crust is deeply golden and the loaf makes a hollow sound when tapped on the bottom. Immediately remove the bread from the Dutch oven and let it cool completely on a rack at room temperature.

VIENNOISERIE

Laminating Butter

Active time
5 minutes

Chilling time
15 minutes

Storage
Up to 12 hours

Equipment
Parchment paper
Rolling pin

Ingredients
Butter, preferably 84% fat
(see Chefs' Notes p. 63)
Flour for dusting

CHEFS' NOTES

This butter is known in French as *beurre de tourage*.

1 • Fold a piece of parchment paper measuring 12 × 16 in. (30 × 40 cm) in half lengthwise to obtain an 8 × 12-in. (20 × 30-cm) rectangle.

2 • Fold this rectangle in three to create a 4 × 8-in. (10 × 20-cm) rectangle, creasing the folds well.

3 • Unfold the paper and place the butter in one of the rectangles toward the center.

CHEFS' NOTES

You will need one-third of the weight of the dough in butter.
For instance, if you have 1 lb. (450 g) dough, you'll need 1 stick + 2 tbsp (5.25 oz./150 g) butter.

4 • Dust the butter with flour and pound with a rolling pin to flatten. The butter should come within about ¼ in. (5 mm) of the fold markings, without going beyond them.

5 • Refold the paper around the butter, following the creases.

6 • Roll the butter until it fills the parchment rectangle and is uniformly thick.

7 • Chill the butter for at least 15 minutes before using.

Making a Single Turn in Puff Pastry

Ingredients
Puff pastry dough (see technique p. 66) and flour for dusting

1 • Dust the work surface very lightly with flour. Roll the dough into a rectangle that is roughly three times as long as it is wide.

2 • Fold the bottom third of the dough upward, then fold the top third down over the top.

3 • The dough is now folded in three, which is known as a single turn.

Making a Double Turn in Puff Pastry

Ingredients
Puff pastry dough (see technique p. 66) and flour for dusting

CHEFS' NOTES

• Mark the dough lightly with your finger for each turn so you can keep track of how many turns you have made.

• This folding technique is also called a "wallet" turn (*tour portefeuille*).

1 • Dust the work surface very lightly with flour. Roll the dough into a rectangle that is roughly three times as long as it is wide.

2 • Fold the shorter ends of the dough inward, one-third of the way down from the top and two-thirds of the way up from the bottom.

3 • Fold the dough in half. The dough is now folded in four, which is known as a double turn.

Classic Puff Pastry

Makes 1 lb. 5 oz. (600 g)

Active time
2 hours

Chilling time
About 1¾ hours

Storage
Up to 3 days in the refrigerator, well wrapped

Ingredients

Water dough (*détrempe*)
1 tsp (5 g) salt
½ cup (125 g/125 ml) water
2 cups (9 oz./250 g) strong white bread flour (T65), sifted
2 tbsp (25 g) butter, melted and cooled

1¾ sticks (7 oz./200 g) butter, preferably 84% butterfat, well chilled

1 • In a mixing bowl, mix together the salt and water. Add the flour and melted butter.

CHEFS' NOTES

• If you add a dash of white vinegar to the water when making the initial dough, it will prevent oxidation and extend the storage time by several days.

• Mark the dough lightly with your finger for each turn so you can keep track of how many turns you have made.

2 • Using a pastry scraper, work the ingredients together until they form a dough, taking care not to overwork it. This water dough is known as the *détrempe*.

3 • Gather the dough together and shape it into a ball.

4 • Using a knife, cut a criss-cross pattern in the dough to relax it.

5 • Cover in plastic wrap and chill in the refrigerator for at least 20 minutes.

6 • Using a rolling pin, soften the butter containing 84% fat, which is to be incorporated into the dough during the folding process. Shape the butter into a square—it should still be cold but needs to be as malleable as the dough you have just made (see technique p. 62).

↪

Classic Puff Pastry (continued)

7 • Roll out the dough so it is twice as long as the square of butter.

8 • Place the butter on the dough and wrap the dough around it to enclose it completely.

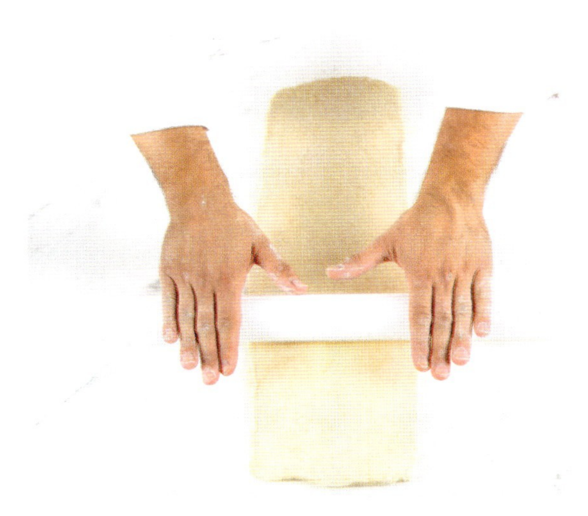

9 • Dust the work surface very lightly with flour and roll the dough into a rectangle measuring 10 × 24 in. (25 × 60 cm).

10 • Fold the dough in three: this is known as a single turn (see technique p. 64). Rotate the folded dough 90° to the right.

11 • Roll out the dough again and fold in three, giving it another single turn. Cover the folded dough with plastic wrap and chill in the refrigerator for 30–40 minutes. At this stage, the dough has been given 2 turns.

12 • Place the chilled dough on the floured work surface, making sure the flap is on one side.

13 • Repeat steps 9–12, so the dough has been given 4 turns. Repeat steps 9–10 for the 5th and final turn. Cover in plastic wrap and chill for 30–40 minutes before using.

CHEFS' NOTES

• As a general rule, puff pastry needs to be given 5 or 6 turns. For the optimum rise, give the dough 5 turns.

• Puff pastry made with 4 turns can be used for puff-pastry straws, while 6 turns are needed for vol-au-vents.

Inverse Puff Pastry

Makes 2 lb. (900 g)

Active time

2 hours

Chilling time

About 2¾ hours

Storage

Up to 4 days in the refrigerator, well wrapped

Ingredients

Beurre manié

1 cup (4.5 oz./130 g) flour

3½ sticks (14 oz./400 g) butter, preferably 84% butterfat, well chilled

Water dough (*détrempe*)

2 cups plus 2 tbsp (9.5 oz./270 g) strong white bread flour (T65)

½ cup plus 1 tbsp (140 g/140 ml) water

1¼ tsp (6 g) salt

1 • Work the flour and butter together with your hands to make the beurre manié (the French term for a flour and butter paste).

2 • Roll the beurre manié into a rectangle, cover with plastic wrap, and chill in the refrigerator for about 20 minutes.

3 • To make the water dough, shape the flour into a mound on a cool surface and make a well in the center. Pour the water into the well and add the salt.

4 • Working with your fingertips, gradually draw the flour into the well so it absorbs the water.

5 • Using a pastry scraper, work the ingredients together to make a smooth dough.

6 • Gather the dough together and shape into a ball. Make criss-cross cuts in the top of the dough with a knife to relax it. Cover with plastic wrap and chill for about 20 minutes.

↪

Inverse Puff Pastry (continued)

7 • Roll the dough into a rectangle measuring 8 × 12 in. (20 × 30 cm). Soften the beurre manié with a rolling pin and roll into a rectangle the same width but twice the length of the dough (see Chefs' Notes p. 73). Place the dough on the beurre manié.

8 • Enclose the dough by folding the beurre manié over it, pressing down firmly on all sides to seal the edges.

9 • Lightly dust the work surface with flour. Roll the dough into a rectangle measuring 10 × 24 in. (25 × 60 cm).

10 • Fold the dough in four to make a double turn (see technique p. 65). Cover in plastic wrap and chill for 30–40 minutes.

11 • Place the dough on a floured work surface, making sure the flap is on one side. Roll it out and fold in four again. At this stage, the dough has undergone 4 turns. Cover in plastic wrap and chill for 30–40 minutes.

12 • Making sure the flap is on one side, roll out the dough again and fold in three, to make a single turn (see technique p. 64). This is the 5th and final turn. Cover in plastic wrap and chill for 30–40 minutes before using.

CHEFS' NOTES

It is important that the butter stays cold but has the same malleability as the water dough (*détrempe*).

Yeasted Puff Pastry

Makes 1 lb. 5 oz. (600 g)

Active time
2 hours

Rising time
15 minutes

Freezing time
1 hour 15 minutes

Chilling time
15 minutes

Storage (water dough, before adding laminated butter)
Up to 12 hours, well covered in plastic wrap

Equipment
Stand mixer + dough hook
Instant-read thermometer

Ingredients

Water dough (*détrempe*)

1 cup (4.25 oz./125 g) all-purpose flour (*gruau*)
1 cup (4.25 oz./125 g) strong white bread flour (T65)
Generous ½ cup (135 g/135 ml) water at 39°F (4°C)
1 tbsp (15 g) milk powder
2½ tbsp (1 oz./30 g) sugar
2 tsp (10 g) butter
0.5 oz. (12 g) fresh yeast
1 tsp (5 g) salt

1 stick + 2 tbsp (5.25 oz./150 g) butter, preferably 84% butterfat, well chilled

1 • Knead all the water dough ingredients together in the bowl of the stand mixer on low speed until well combined.

2 • Increase the speed to high and knead until the dough is smooth and elastic. The dough temperature should be 70°F–73°F (21°C–23°C). Shape the dough into a ball, cover with plastic wrap, and let rise for 15 minutes at room temperature.

3 • Roll the dough into a rectangle measuring 8 × 12 in. (20 × 30 cm), with a thickness of ¼ in. (6 mm). Cover with plastic wrap and freeze for 30 minutes.

4 • Roll the 84% butter into a 6 × 8-in. (15 × 20-cm) rectangle (see technique p. 62). Chill for 15 minutes, then place the butter in the center of the chilled dough.

5 • Fold the dough over to enclose the butter completely.

6 • Using a knife, make a vertical cut on each side of the dough.

↪

Yeasted Puff Pastry (continued)

7 • Roll the dough into an 8 × 24-in. (20 × 60-cm) rectangle, with a thickness of ¼ in. (6 mm).

8 • Fold the shorter ends of the dough toward the center, two-thirds of the way up from the bottom and one-third of the way down from the top.

9 • Fold the dough in half to make a double turn. Freeze for 15 minutes.

10 • Make a vertical cut on each side of the dough, then repeat steps 7 to 9. Freeze for 30 minutes before using.

Croissants

Makes 8

Active time
15 minutes

Proofing time
2–2½ hours

Chilling time (optional)
5 minutes

Cooking time
15 minutes

Storage
A few hours in a paper bag or wrapped in a clean dish towel

Equipment
Chef's knife
Pastry brush

Ingredients
1 lb. 5 oz. (600 g) yeasted puff pastry dough (see technique p. 74)

Egg wash
1 egg
1 egg yolk
2 tsp (10 g/10 ml) whole milk

1 • Roll out the dough to a thickness of ⅛ in. (4 mm) and cut out a 12 × 16½-in. (30 × 40-cm) rectangle. Cut into 4 rectangles with 4-in. (10-cm) bases.

2 • Cut each rectangle in half diagonally to obtain triangles.

3 • Roll each triangle up from the base to the tip, taking care not to press too hard and squash the dough.

↪

Croissants (continued)

4 • Flatten the tip and tuck it under the croissant to stabilize it (see Chefs' Notes).

5 • Place the croissants on a nonstick baking sheet. Whisk the egg wash ingredients together and brush evenly over the tops. Place a bowl of boiling water in a cool oven (79°F/26°C), place the croissants above, and let proof for 2–2½ hours.

6 • Preheat the oven on fan setting to 340°F (170°C/Gas Mark 3). Brush again with the egg wash, then bake for about 15 minutes.

CHEFS' NOTES

• Flattening the tips and tucking them under the croissants before proofing and baking makes them less likely to unwind.

• To firm up the dough after proofing, you can chill the croissants for 5 minutes before applying the egg wash a second time: they will be less fragile.

Chocolate Croissants (*Pains au chocolat*)

Makes 8

Active time
15 minutes

Proofing time
2–2½ hours

Chilling time (optional)
5 minutes

Cooking time
15 minutes

Storage
A few hours in a paper bag or wrapped in a clean dish towel

Equipment
Chef's knife
Pastry brush

Ingredients
1 lb. 5 oz. (600 g) yeasted puff pastry dough (see technique p. 74)
16 × 3-in. (8-cm) *pain au chocolat* sticks

Egg wash
1 egg
1 egg yolk
2 tsp (10 g/10 ml) whole milk

1 • Roll out the dough to a thickness of ⅛ in. (3 mm) and cut out a 12 × 12½-in. (30 × 32-cm) rectangle. Cut in half to form rectangles measuring 6 × 12½ in. (15 × 32 cm).

2 • Place 2 rows of chocolate sticks along one long edge of each rectangle, leaving ¼ in. (5 mm) between the first row and the edge of the rectangle and between the 2 rows. Cut the dough vertically after each chocolate stick, to form 8 rectangles measuring 3 × 6 in. (8 × 15 cm) each.

3 • Start by rolling the top of the dough over the first chocolate stick, then roll up the rest.

↪

Chocolate Croissants (continued)

4 • Using the palm of your hand, press down lightly to seal the joint underneath, ensuring it is in the center. Place the chocolate croissants on a nonstick baking sheet.

5 • Whisk the egg wash ingredients together and brush evenly over the tops. Place a bowl of boiling water in a cool oven (79°F/26°C), place the chocolate croissants above, and let proof for 2–2½ hours.

6 • Preheat the oven on fan setting to 340°F (170°C/Gas Mark 3). Brush again with the egg wash, then bake for about 15 minutes.

CHEFS' NOTES

To firm up the dough after proofing, you can chill the chocolate croissants for 5 minutes before applying the egg wash a second time: they will be less fragile.

Raisin Swirls (*Pains aux raisins*)

Makes 8

Active time
15 minutes

Proofing time
1½–2 hours

Cooking time
20 minutes

Storage
A few hours in a paper bag or wrapped in a clean dish towel

Equipment
Offset palette knife
Serrated knife
Pastry brush

Ingredients
1 lb. 5 oz. (600 g) yeasted puff pastry dough (see technique p. 74)
6.25 oz. (180 g) pastry cream (see technique p. 112)
Scant 1 cup (4.25 oz./120 g) raisins, soaked for 1 hour in boiling water or 2½ tbsp (40 g/40 ml) alcohol or flavoring of your choice, such as rum, kirsch, or orange-flower water

Glaze
⅓ cup (2.75 oz./75 g) sugar
3½ tbsp (50 g/50 ml) water

1 • Roll out the dough to a thickness of ⅛ in. (3 mm) and cut out a 10½ × 17¾-in. (27 × 45-cm) rectangle. Flatten the short end facing you and, using the offset palette knife, spread the pastry cream in a thin, even layer over the rest of the dough.

2 • Drain the raisins and scatter them evenly over the pastry cream.

↪

Raisin Swirls (continued)

3 • Brush the flattened border of the dough with a little water to seal the swirls. Carefully roll the dough up lengthwise toward you, with the filling inside.

4 • Ensuring the seam is underneath, cut the roll into 8 slices measuring approximately 1¼ in. (3 cm), using the serrated knife.

5 • Place the slices flat on a nonstick baking sheet. Place a bowl of boiling water in a cool oven (79°F/26°C), place the raisin swirls above, and let them proof for 1½–2 hours.

6 • Preheat the oven on fan setting to 325°F (160°C/Gas Mark 3). Bake the swirls for about 20 minutes. For the glaze, dissolve the sugar in the water and bring to a boil. Remove the swirls from the oven and brush immediately with glaze.

Apple Turnovers (*Chaussons aux pommes*)

Makes 5

Active time
30 minutes

Chilling time
30 minutes

Cooking time
30 minutes

Storage
Up to 24 hours in a paper bag or wrapped in a clean dish towel

Equipment
Fluted oval-shaped 5 × 6-in. (12 × 16-cm) cookie cutter
Pastry brush
Paring knife

Ingredients
1 lb. 5 oz. (600 g) inverse puff pastry dough (see technique p. 70), well chilled
14 oz. (400 g) apple compote (see technique p. 116)

Egg wash
1 egg
1 egg yolk
2 tsp (10 g/10 ml) whole milk

Simple syrup made with 3½ tbsp (50 g/50 ml) water and ⅓ cup (2.75 oz./75 g) sugar, cooled

1 • Roll the dough into a 7 × 24-in. (18 × 60-cm) rectangle. Cut out 5 ovals using the cutter.

2 • Using a rolling pin, gently roll the middle part of each oval to make an elongated shape about 8 in. (20 cm) long, without flattening the edges.

3 • Brush a little water along the edge of the bottom half of each pastry oval.

↪

Apple Turnovers (continued)

4 • Place a mound of apple compote in the center of each bottom half. Fold the pastry over the filling and press the edges together to seal firmly.

5 • Place the turnovers on a baking sheet lined with parchment paper. Whisk together the egg wash ingredients and brush over the turnovers. Chill for 30 minutes.

6 • Preheat the oven to 375°F (190°C/Gas Mark 5). Brush the turnovers again with egg wash and score an attractive pattern in the dough using the tip of the paring knife.

CHEFS' NOTES

• Make sure the dough is cold when you work with it. If it starts to get warm and sticky, place it in the refrigerator or freezer for a few minutes, to firm it up.

• You can freeze the turnovers before cooking them. Bake without thawing, adding 7 minutes to the baking time.

7 • Bake for 30 minutes, until crisp and golden. As soon as the turnovers come out of the oven, brush with the syrup.

Palmiers

Makes 10

Active time
30 minutes

Freezing time
1 hour

Cooking time
20 minutes

Storage
Up to 3 days in an airtight container

Equipment
Chef's knife

Ingredients
1 lb. 5 oz. (600 g) inverse puff pastry dough, made up to 2 turns (see technique p. 70)
2/3 cup (4 1/2 oz./125 g) superfine sugar

1 • Place the dough on a work surface sprinkled with sugar and give it a double turn (see technique p. 65), sprinkling it liberally with sugar. Give the dough a single turn (see technique p. 64), sprinkling it with more sugar.

↪

Palmiers (continued)

2 • Roll the dough into a 6 × 27½-in. (15 × 70-cm) rectangle. Using the chef's knife, trim the ends to obtain neat edges.

3 • Fold the two short ends in toward the center so they almost meet (leave a finger-width gap between them). Flatten lightly with a rolling pin.

4 • Fold the dough in half and place in the freezer for 1 hour. Remove from the freezer and cut into slices about ½ in. (1 cm) thick. Preheat the oven to 350°F (180°C/Gas Mark 4) and line a baking sheet with parchment paper.

5 • Place the palmiers on the baking sheet. Bake for about 20 minutes, turning them over after about 10 minutes, when they are brown and caramelized, to brown the other side. When baked, transfer immediately to a rack to cool.

Brioche Dough

Makes 1 lb. 5 oz. (600 g)

Active time
30 minutes

Bulk fermentation time
30 minutes

Chilling time
2 hours minimum
(ideally overnight)

Storage
Up to 2 days in the refrigerator

Equipment
Stand mixer + dough hook
Bowl scraper

Ingredients
2 cups (9 oz./250 g) all-purpose flour (*gruau*)
½ cup (4.5 oz./125 g) lightly beaten egg (about 2½ eggs), well chilled
1½ tbsp (25 g/25 ml) whole milk
3 tbsp (1.25 oz./35 g) superfine sugar
1 tsp (5 g) salt
0.25 oz. (8 g) fresh yeast
3 tbsp (1.75 oz./50 g) crème fraîche or heavy cream
1 stick + 1 tsp (4.25 oz./120 g) butter, diced, at room temperature

1 • Using your hands, roughly combine all the ingredients, except the butter, in the bowl of the stand mixer.

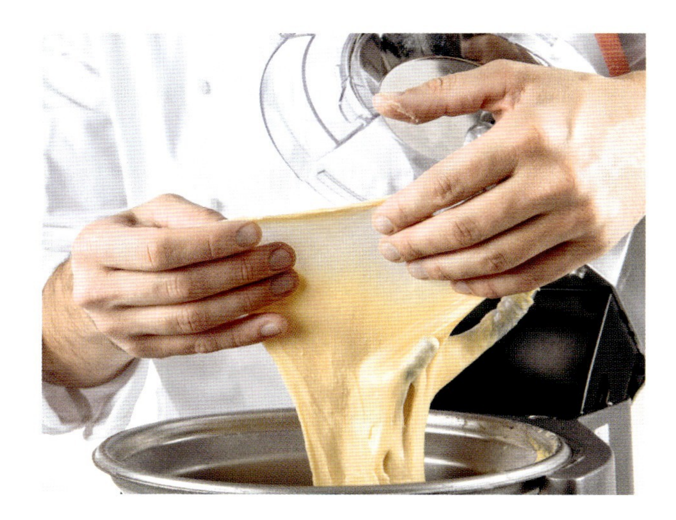

2 • Using the dough hook, knead at low speed for 5 minutes. Increase the speed to medium and knead for 15 minutes, until the dough pulls away from the sides of the bowl, scraping down the sides regularly. The dough should be elastic.

3 • Gradually knead in the butter. When incorporated, knead for 5 minutes, until the dough pulls away from the sides of the bowl.

4 • Shape the dough into a ball, transfer to a clean bowl, and cover with plastic wrap. Let ferment at room temperature for 30 minutes.

5 • Give the dough several folds to burst any air bubbles trapped inside and make the dough stronger (see technique p. 48). Cover and chill for at least 2 hours (or ideally overnight) before using.

Large Parisian Brioche

Makes 1 large (10½-oz./300-g) brioche to serve 4

Active time
10 minutes

Proofing time
1½ hours

Cooking time
20 minutes

Storage
Up to 2 days

Equipment
6⅓-in. (16-cm) brioche mold
Pastry brush

Ingredients
10.5 oz. (300 g) brioche dough (see technique p. 90)
Softened butter for the mold

Egg wash
1 egg
1 egg yolk
2 tsp (10 g/10 ml) whole milk

1 • Cut the dough into 5 squares weighing slightly under 1.75 oz. (48 g) and 1 square weighing 2 oz. (60 g).

2 • Fold the corners of the larger square in toward the center.

3 • Once all the corners have been folded in, turn the piece over so the seam faces downward.

4 • Roll it against the work surface between your palm and thumb to shape it into a ball.

5 • Do the same with the other 5 dough squares.

6 • Using the pastry brush, thoroughly grease the mold with the butter.

↪

Large Parisian Brioche (continued)

7 • Arrange the 5 smaller balls in a ring. Form a teardrop shape with the larger ball and nestle it snugly into the center of the ring with the tip pointing downward.

8 • Carefully transfer to the mold.

9 • Whisk the egg wash ingredients together and lightly brush over the top of the brioche. Place a bowl of boiling water in a cool oven (79°F/26°C), place the brioche above, and let proof for about 1½ hours.

10 • Preheat the oven to 350°F (180°C/Gas Mark 4) and heat a baking sheet. Brush the brioche again with the egg wash. Place on the hot baking sheet to help the "head" rise and bake for 5 minutes. Reduce the temperature to 330°F (165°C/Gas Mark 3) and bake for 15 minutes. Immediately turn out of the mold to stop it reabsorbing any steam.

Individual Parisian Brioches

Makes 6

Active time
10 minutes

Proofing time
1½ hours

Cooking time
8 minutes

Storage
Up to 2 days

Equipment
Pastry brush
6 × 2½-in. (6-cm) brioche molds

Ingredients
9.5 oz. (270 g) brioche dough
(see technique p. 90)
Softened butter for the molds

Egg wash
1 egg
1 egg yolk
2 tsp (10 g/10 ml) whole milk

1 • Divide the dough into 6 pieces weighing 1 oz. (30 g) each and 6 pieces weighing 0.5 oz. (15 g) each. Roll into balls.

2 • Using the pastry brush, thoroughly grease the molds with the butter. Make holes in the centers of the larger balls to obtain rings.

3 • Form teardrop shapes with the smaller balls. Insert the tips into the rings to make the brioche "heads."

4 • Place the brioches in the molds. Whisk the egg wash ingredients together and gently brush over the brioches. Place a bowl of boiling water in a cool oven (79°F/26°C), place the brioches above, and let proof for about 1½ hours.

5 • Preheat the oven to 425°F (220°C/Gas Mark 7) and heat a baking sheet. Brush the brioches again with egg wash. Place the molds on the hot sheet to help the "heads" rise and bake for 8 minutes.

6 • When baked, immediately turn the brioches out of the molds to stop them reabsorbing any steam.

Brioche Crown

Serves 6

Active time
10 minutes

Resting time
10 minutes

Proofing time
1½ hours

Cooking time
25 minutes

Storage
Up to 24 hours in a paper bag or wrapped in a clean dish towel

Equipment
Pastry brush
Scissors

Ingredients
10.5 oz. (300 g) brioche dough (see technique p. 90), chilled overnight

Egg wash
1 egg
1 egg yolk
2 tsp (10 g/10 ml) whole milk

Decoration
Pearl sugar

1 • Shape the chilled brioche dough into a ball following the technique on p. 50. Let rest in the refrigerator for 10 minutes.

2 • Roll the dough into a 10-in. (25-cm) disk and make a hole in the center using your finger.

3 • Slowly stretch the hole to make it bigger, taking care not to tear the dough.

4 • Gently fold the inside edge of the hole outward.

5 • Roll this new sausage-shaped fold under the palm of your hand to obtain an even and well-rounded shape. Let the dough relax for a few minutes if it tears or pulls back too much.

6 • Fold the outer edge of the dough up and over the raised ring.

↪

Brioche Crown (continued)

7 • Stretch and roll the dough to shape it into a crown. Place on a baking sheet lined with parchment paper.

8 • Whisk together the egg wash ingredients and brush over the ring. Place a bowl of boiling water in a cool oven (79°F/26°C), place the baking sheet above, and let the dough proof for about 1½ hours.

9 • Preheat the oven to 300°F (150°C/Gas Mark 2). Brush the dough again with egg wash. Using the scissors, cut incisions at regular intervals around the top.

10 • Sprinkle with pearl sugar and bake for 25 minutes.

Shaping a Single-Strand Braid

Ingredients
Brioche dough

1 • Place a strand of dough, 16 in. (40 cm) long, vertically on the work surface and mark lightly into three roughly equal parts.

2 • Coil the top two-thirds of the strand around in a circle, making sure the tip rests on the strand.

3 • Pass the tip of the remaining third through the loop, taking it over then under the strand.

4 • Holding the rounded end of the loop, twist it to make a figure 8.

5 • Pass the loose end of the dough through the newly created loop.

6 • Pinch the ends together.

Shaping a Two-Strand Braid

Ingredients
Brioche dough

1 • Arrange two strands of dough, each 20–24 in. (50–60 cm) long, in a cross shape, placing the vertical strand over the horizontal one.

2 • Fold the left-hand side of the horizontal strand over the vertical strand, placing it parallel with and just below the right-hand side of the strand.

3 • Fold the original right-hand side of the horizontal strand over the vertical strand, to form a cross.

4 • Repeat with the vertical strand, folding the top strand down over the horizontal strand and placing it parallel with and to the right of the bottom strand. Fold the bottom strand up over the horizontal strand.

5 • Repeat steps 2–4 until you reach the end of the strand, following the same order every time.

6 • Pinch the ends together to finish the two-strand braid.

Shaping a Three-Strand Braid

Ingredients
Brioche dough

CHEFS' NOTES

Take care not to make the braid too tight—you should be able to see the work surface between the plaits. This leaves enough room for the dough to expand and prevents it from tearing when baking.

1 • Place three strands of dough with pointed tips on the work surface and pinch them together at one end. With the open ends facing you, place two strands to the right and the third to the left.

2 • Lift the rightmost strand up and over the second, and set it down just inside the third.

3 • Pick up the leftmost strand.

4 • Pass it over the middle strand and set it down just inside the strand on the right.

5 • Repeat steps 2–4 until you reach the end.

6 • Be sure to keep the braid flat.

7 • Pinch the ends of the strands together to finish the braid.

Milk Bread Rolls (*Navettes*)

Makes 10

Active time
1 hour

Bulk fermentation time
45 minutes

Proofing time
1½ hours

Cooking time
6 minutes

Storage
Up to 24 hours in a paper bag or wrapped in a clean dish towel

Equipment
Stand mixer + dough hook
Bowl scraper
Pastry brush
Scissors

Ingredients
2 cups (9 oz./250 g) all-purpose flour (*gruau*)
¼ cup + 1 tsp (2 oz./65 g) lightly beaten egg (about 1½ eggs)
⅓ cup (75 g/75 ml) whole milk
2½ tbsp (1 oz./30 g) sugar
1 tsp (5 g) salt
0.35 oz. (10 g) fresh yeast
4 tbsp (2.5 oz./65 g) butter, diced, at room temperature

Egg wash
1 egg
1 egg yolk
2 tsp (10 g/10 ml) whole milk

Decoration
Pearl sugar

1 • Make a brioche dough using the ingredients listed (see technique p. 90). In step 4, let the dough ferment at room temperature for 45 minutes, then firmly flatten to burst any air bubbles. Cut into 10 pieces weighing 1.75 oz. (55 g) each. Flatten to remove air bubbles. Fold the top two-thirds down, then fold the bottom two-thirds up. Fold in half to seal.

2 • Roll each piece of dough against the work surface into 4-in. (10-cm) logs with pointed ends (known as *navettes* in French, as they resemble small boats). Place on a baking sheet lined with parchment paper.

3 • Whisk the egg wash ingredients together and brush over the rolls. Place a bowl of boiling water in a cool oven (79°F/26°C), place the baking sheet above, and let the dough proof for about 1½ hours.

4 • Preheat the oven to 425°F (220°C/Gas Mark 7). Brush the rolls again with the egg wash. Dip the scissors in water and cut a small wheat stalk pattern down their length.

5 • Sprinkle with pearl sugar and bake for 6 minutes until golden.

CREAMS AND FILLINGS

Pastry Cream

Makes scant 3½ cups (1¾ lb./800 g)

Active time
15 minutes

Cooking time
2–3 minutes

Storage
Up to 24 hours in the refrigerator

Ingredients

2 cups (500 g/500 ml) whole milk
½ cup (3.5 oz./100 g) sugar, divided
1 vanilla bean, split lengthwise
Scant ½ cup (3.5 oz./100 g) egg (about 2 eggs)
2 tbsp (25 g) cornstarch
2 tbsp (25 g) flour
3½ tbsp (1.75 oz./50 g) butter, diced, at room temperature

Flavorings

Coffee: Add 1–1½ tbsp (15–20 ml) coffee extract or 1 tbsp (0.5 oz./15 g) instant coffee to the milk, or steep ¾ cup (2.5 oz./70 g) ground coffee in the milk, and then strain.

Alcohols: When the cream is cold, mix in the equivalent of 2–3% of the total weight of the cream (about 1 tsp/5 g).

Chocolate: Mix ⅓ cup (1.5 oz./40 g) 100% pure cacao paste into the warm cream.

CHEFS' NOTES

For chocolate-flavored pastry cream, reduce the quantity of flour by 10 to 20% to ensure the cream is not too compact. The 100% pure cacao paste can be replaced with any chocolate of your choice; reduce the amount of sugar in the recipe, so that the cream is not too sweet.

1 • Combine the milk and half of the sugar in a saucepan. Scrape in the seeds of the vanilla bean and bring to a boil over medium heat.

2 • Meanwhile, whisk the egg with the remaining sugar in a mixing bowl until blended and slightly thickened. Sift the cornstarch and flour into the egg mixture and whisk until combined.

CHEFS' NOTES

Use this cream for raisin swirls, frangipane, and various individual cakes and pastries.

3 • As soon as the milk comes to a boil, slowly pour some into the egg and flour mixture, whisking constantly. This will loosen the mixture and heat it a little.

4 • Pour the mixture back into the saucepan and bring to a boil over medium heat, whisking vigorously. Continue to boil, still whisking, for 2–3 minutes.

5 • Remove from the heat and stir in the diced butter until smooth.

6 • To cool the pastry cream quickly, line a baking sheet with plastic wrap and spread the cream over it. Press another piece of plastic wrap over the surface of the cream.

Almond Cream

Makes scant 1 cup (7 oz./200 g)

Active time

20 minutes

Storage

Up to 2 days in the refrigerator

Ingredients

3½ tbsp (1.75 oz./50 g) butter, diced, at room temperature

¼ cup (1.75 oz./50 g) sugar

3–3½ tbsp (1.5–1.75 oz./45–50 g) egg (about 1 egg), at room temperature

½ cup (1.75 oz./50 g) almond flour

1 tsp (5 g) custard powder (see Chefs' Notes below)

1 vanilla bean, split lengthwise

½ tsp (2.5 g/2.5 ml) rum, at room temperature

1 • In a mixing bowl, work the butter with a spatula until it is very soft and smooth.

CHEFS' NOTES

• The custard powder can be replaced by flour, cornstarch, or potato starch.

• Use this cream for frangipane, almond croissants, or as a filling for various tarts, tartlets, and other pastries.

2 • Add the sugar and beat until light and creamy.

3 • Gradually add the egg, stirring until thoroughly incorporated.

4 • Add the almond flour and mix until the cream is smooth. Avoid overbeating, as the extra air beaten in will make the cream swell up during baking.

5 • Add the custard powder, the seeds from the vanilla bean, and the rum, and mix well. Store covered in the refrigerator until ready to use.

CHEFS' NOTES

• When almond cream is used as a filling (for galettes, almond croissants, tarts, etc.), the baking time will need to be increased.

• Avoid excessive beating, as too much air will cause the almond cream to puff up during baking.

Apple Compote

Makes 1 lb. 2 oz. (500 g)

Active time
30 minutes

Cooking time
8–10 minutes

Storage
Up to 3 days in the refrigerator, well covered with plastic wrap

Equipment
Vegetable peeler
Paring knife

Ingredients
1 lb. 2 oz. (500 g) apples
2 tbsp (25 g) butter
2 tbsp (25 g) sugar, depending on the tartness of the apples

1 • Peel the apples using the peeler, then cut them in half and remove the stems.

2 • Using the tip of the paring knife, cut out the seeds and core.

3 • Cut the apples into approximately ½-in. (1-cm) dice.

4 • Melt the butter in a saucepan over medium heat.

5 • Add the apples and cook until softened (about 5 minutes). Stir in the sugar and continue cooking until the apples are tender and caramelized (about 3–5 minutes).

Praline Paste

Makes 1 lb. 2 oz. (500 g)

Active time
40 minutes

Cooking time
15 minutes

Storage
Up to 2 weeks, well covered in plastic wrap, in an airtight container

Equipment
Copper pan
Candy thermometer
Nonstick baking sheet or silicone baking mat
Food processor

Ingredients
1⅓ cups (9 oz./250 g) sugar
Scant ½ cup (100 g/100 ml) water
4.5 oz. (125 g) blanched almonds, unroasted
4.5 oz. (125 g) skinned hazelnuts, unroasted

1 • Add the sugar to the water in the copper pan, heat until the sugar has dissolved, and cook to 243°F (117°C): the firm-ball stage.

2 • Add the nuts and stir well using a spatula until the sugar becomes opaque and starts to crystallize.

3 • The sugar crystals will stick to the nuts, so continue cooking and stirring until the sugar caramelizes and, at the same time, the nuts become roasted.

4 • To check the nuts are sufficiently roasted, carefully lift one out and cut it in half. When the mixture is ready, transfer it to a nonstick baking sheet or silicone baking mat.

5 • When cool, break the caramelized nuts roughly into large chunks and place in a food processor.

6 • Process to a smooth paste.

CHEFS' NOTES

• Take care not to roast the nuts or cook the caramel for too long, as allowing them to darken too much will impart an unpleasant bitter flavor to the praline.

• For extra flavor, add ½ vanilla bean to the cooked sugar with the nuts and leave it in when you process the praline to a paste.

• You can also add the finely grated zest of a lemon just before processing.

Chocolate Spread

Makes 6 × 1-cup (250-ml) jars

Active time
15 minutes

Setting time
1 hour

Storage
Up to 2 weeks in the refrigerator

Equipment
Instant-read thermometer
6 × 1-cup (250-ml) jars

Ingredients
6 oz. (175 g) milk couverture chocolate, 46% cacao
1 lb. 12 oz. (785 g) hazelnut praline, 55% hazelnuts
3 tbsp (1.5 oz./40 g) clarified butter

CHEFS' NOTES

Remove the jar of spread from the refrigerator about 1 hour before serving, to ensure a spreadable consistency.

1 • In a bowl over a saucepan of barely simmering water (bain-marie), heat the chocolate to 113°F–122°F (45°C–50°C), then pour it over the hazelnut praline.

2 • Using a flexible spatula, mix well to combine. Stir in the clarified butter and mix thoroughly until a smooth texture is obtained.

3 • Pour into the jars and let cool before closing them. Place in the refrigerator to set.

Béchamel Sauce

Makes 2 cups (1 lb. 2 oz./500 g)

Active time

15 minutes

Storage

Up to 2 days in the refrigerator, covered with plastic wrap pressed against the surface

Equipment

Whisk

Flexible spatula

Ingredients

3 tbsp (1.75 oz./50 g) butter

Scant ½ cup (1.75 oz./50 g) all-purpose flour

2 cups (500 g/500 ml) whole milk

1 pinch ground nutmeg

Salt and freshly ground pepper

1 • Melt the butter in a saucepan over medium heat.

2 • Make a roux by adding the flour all at once, whisking constantly until no lumps remain.

3 • Gradually pour in the milk, whisking continually over medium heat to prevent sticking. Cook until thickened.

4 • Remove from the heat, add the nutmeg, and season with salt and pepper.

5 • Transfer the béchamel sauce to a bowl to cool it down, stirring occasionally with the spatula to prevent a skin forming. Press plastic wrap against the surface and chill until using.

RECIPES

CLASSIC BREADS

TRADITIONAL POOLISH BAGUETTES

Baguette de tradition sur poolish

Makes 5 baguettes, weighing 7 oz. (200 g) each

Active time

1½ hours

Poolish fermentation time

4 hours

Autolyse time

30 minutes–1 hour

Bulk fermentation time

1 hour

Resting time

30 minutes

Proofing time

45 minutes–1 hour

Cooking time

20 minutes

Storage

Up to 24 hours rolled up in a clean dish towel, or parbake and freeze (see p. 21)

Equipment

Stand mixer + dough hook

Instant-read thermometer

Baker's couche (optional)

Heavy-duty baking sheet or baking stone

Bread lame

Ingredients

Poolish

0.05 oz. (1 g) fresh yeast, crumbled

Scant ½ cup (100 g/100 ml) water

¾ cup + 2 tbsp (3.5 oz./100 g) white bread flour (T65)

Scant ½ tsp (2 g) salt

Baguette dough

4 cups + 2 tbsp (1 lb. 2 oz./500 g) white bread flour (T65)

1¼ cups (300 g/300 ml) water

Poolish (see above)

0.1 oz. (2 g) fresh yeast

1¾ tsp (9 g) salt

2 tsp (10 g/10 ml) water (for *bassinage*)

PREPARING THE POOLISH

Whisk the yeast into the water until it has dissolved completely. Whisk in the flour and salt until well combined and smooth. Cover with plastic wrap and let ferment for 4 hours at room temperature.

PREPARING THE BAGUETTE DOUGH

Knead the flour and water in the bowl of the stand mixer on low speed for 5 minutes until no dry bits remain. Cover the bowl with plastic wrap and let rest for 30 minutes–1 hour at room temperature (autolyse). Add the poolish, yeast, and salt, and knead on low speed for 10 minutes, followed by 2 minutes on high speed, until the dough is supple, smooth, and elastic. With the mixer running on low speed, gradually add the 2 tsp (10 g/10 ml) water, then increase the speed to high until the water is absorbed and the dough is smooth (*bassinage*). Make sure the dough temperature does not exceed 77°F (25°C). Place in a clean bowl, cover with plastic wrap, and let ferment for 1 hour at room temperature. Fold the dough once halfway through the rise time, after 30 minutes (see technique p. 48). Divide the dough into 5 pieces weighing 7 oz. (200 g) each, and gently shape each one into a ball. Let rest for 30 minutes at room temperature.

SHAPING AND PROOFING THE DOUGH

Shape each piece of dough into a 12-in. (30-cm) baguette (see technique p. 51). Place the baguettes seam side down on a floured baker's couche or thick dish towel and pleat the couche or towel like an accordion between them to maintain their shape. Let proof for 45 minutes–1 hour at room temperature in a draft-free place.

SCORING AND BAKING THE BAGUETTES

Place a heavy-duty baking sheet or baking stone on a rack in the center of the oven and an empty heavy-duty rimmed baking sheet on the bottom rack. Preheat the oven to 515°F (270°C/Gas Mark 10) and bring 1 cup (250 ml) water to a simmer. Transfer the baguettes to a sheet of parchment paper. Using the bread lame, score the baguettes, making 3 cuts in each (see technique p. 54). Slide the baguettes, still on the parchment paper, onto the hot baking sheet or baking stone in the center of the oven and carefully pour the simmering water into the rimmed sheet on the lower rack to create steam. Quickly close the oven door and bake for 20 minutes. If you want a thick, crisp crust, lower the oven temperature to 400°F (200°C/Gas Mark 6), open the door to release the steam, and then close it again. Leave the baguettes to dry for 5–10 minutes. Immediately transfer the baguettes to a rack and let them cool completely at room temperature.

RUSTIC SOURDOUGH BAGUETTES

Baguette rustique au levain T80

Makes 5 baguettes, weighing 6.75 oz. (190 g) each

Active time

1½ hours

Autolyse time

1 hour

Bulk fermentation time

1 hour + overnight

Resting time

45 minutes

Proofing time

45 minutes–1 hour

Cooking time

About 20 minutes

Storage

Up to 24 hours rolled up in a clean dish towel, or parbake and freeze (see p. 21)

Equipment

Stand mixer + dough hook

Instant-read thermometer

Baker's couche (optional)

Heavy-duty baking sheet or baking stone

Bread lame

Ingredients

Scant 4½ cups (1 lb. 2 oz./500 g) stoneground white whole wheat flour (T80)

Scant 1½ cups (350 g/350 ml) water

2.5 oz. (75 g) young stiff levain (see technique p. 38)

2 tsp (10 g) salt

5 tsp (25 g/25 ml) water (*bassinage*)

PREPARING THE BAGUETTE DOUGH (1 DAY AHEAD)

Knead the flour and water in the bowl of the stand mixer on low speed for 5 minutes until no dry bits remain. Cover the bowl with plastic wrap and let rest for 1 hour at room temperature (autolyse). Add the levain and salt and knead on low speed for 10 minutes, followed by 2 minutes on high speed, until the dough is supple, smooth, and elastic. With the mixer running on low speed, add the 5 tsp (25 g/25 ml) water in 3 equal quantities and knead until the dough is smooth: it should be soft and supple but not wet. Make sure the dough temperature does not exceed 73°F–75°F (23°C–24°C). Place in a clean bowl, cover with plastic wrap, and let ferment for 1 hour at room temperature. Fold the dough once (see technique p. 48), cover with plastic wrap, and let ferment overnight in the refrigerator.

SHAPING AND PROOFING THE DOUGH

The next day, divide the dough into 5 pieces weighing 6.75 oz. (190 g) each, and gently shape each one into a ball. Let rest for 45 minutes at room temperature. Shape each piece of dough into a baguette (see technique p. 51). Place the baguettes seam side up on a floured baker's couche or thick dish towel and pleat the couche or towel like an accordion between them to maintain their shape. Let proof for 45 minutes–1 hour at room temperature in a draft-free place.

SCORING AND BAKING THE BAGUETTES

Place a heavy-duty baking sheet or baking stone on a rack in the center of the oven and an empty heavy-duty rimmed baking sheet on the bottom rack. Preheat the oven to 515°F (270°C/Gas Mark 10) and bring 1 cup (250 ml) water to a simmer. Invert the baguettes onto parchment paper and score them lengthwise down the center. Slide the baguettes, still on the parchment paper, onto the hot baking sheet or baking stone in the center of the oven and carefully pour the simmering water into the rimmed sheet on the lower rack to create steam. Quickly close the oven door and bake for about 18 minutes. If you want a thick, crisp crust, lower the oven temperature to 400°F (200°C/Gas Mark 6), open the door to release the steam, and then close it again. Leave the baguettes to dry for 5–10 minutes. Immediately transfer the baguettes to a rack and let them cool completely at room temperature.

MULTISEED POOLISH BAGUETTES

Baguette aux graines

Makes 6 baguettes, weighing about 7 oz. (200 g) each

Active time

1½ hours

Poolish fermentation time

4 hours

Autolyse time

30 minutes–1 hour

Bulk fermentation time

1 hour

Resting time

30 minutes

Proofing time

45 minutes–1 hour

Cooking time

20 minutes

Storage

Up to 24 hours rolled up in a clean dish towel, or parbake and freeze (see p. 21)

Equipment

Stand mixer + dough hook

Instant-read thermometer

Baker's couche (optional)

Heavy-duty baking sheet or baking stone

Bread lame

Ingredients

Toasted seeds

3 tbsp (25 g) sesame seeds

3 tbsp (25 g) sunflower seeds

3 tbsp (25 g) poppy seeds

3 tbsp (25 g) flaxseed

Poolish

0.05 oz. (1 g) fresh yeast, crumbled

¾ cup (175 g/175 ml) water

¾ cup + 2 tbsp (3.5 oz./100 g) white bread flour (T65)

Toasted seeds (see above)

Scant ½ tsp (2 g) salt

Baguette dough

4 cups + 2 tbsp (1 lb. 2 oz./500 g) white bread flour (T65)

1¼ cups (300 g/300 ml) water

Poolish (see above)

0.1 oz. (2 g) fresh yeast

1¾ tsp (9 g) salt

2 tsp (10 g/10 ml) water (for *bassinage*)

TOASTING THE SEEDS

Preheat the oven to 350°F (180°C/Gas Mark 4). Spread all the seeds over a baking sheet lined with parchment paper and toast for about 15 minutes, until fragrant and golden. Let cool to room temperature before using.

PREPARING THE POOLISH

Whisk the yeast into the water until it has dissolved completely. Whisk in the flour, toasted seeds, and salt until well combined. Cover with plastic wrap and let ferment for 4 hours at room temperature.

PREPARING THE BAGUETTE DOUGH

Knead the flour and water in the bowl of the stand mixer on low speed for 5 minutes until no dry bits remain. Cover the bowl with plastic wrap and let rest for 30 minutes–1 hour at room temperature (autolyse). Add the poolish, yeast, and salt and knead on low speed for 10 minutes, followed by 2 minutes on high speed, until the dough is supple, smooth, and elastic. With the mixer running on low speed, gradually add the 2 tsp (10 g/10 ml) water, then increase the speed to high until the water is absorbed and the dough is smooth (*bassinage*). Make sure the dough temperature does not exceed 77°F (25°C). Place in a clean bowl, cover with plastic wrap, and let ferment for 1 hour at room temperature, folding the dough once halfway through, after 30 minutes (see technique p. 48). Divide the dough into 6 pieces weighing 7 oz. (200 g) each, and gently shape each one into a ball. Let rest for 30 minutes at room temperature.

SHAPING AND PROOFING THE DOUGH

Shape each piece of dough into a baguette (see technique p. 51). Place the baguettes seam side up on a floured baker's couche or thick dish towel and pleat the couche or towel like an accordion between them to maintain their shape. Let proof for 45 minutes–1 hour at room temperature in a draft-free place.

SCORING AND BAKING THE BAGUETTES

Place a heavy-duty baking sheet or baking stone on a rack in the center of the oven and a heavy-duty rimmed baking sheet on the bottom rack. Preheat the oven to 500°F (260°C/Gas Mark 10) and bring 1 cup (250 ml) water to a simmer. Place the baguettes on parchment paper and score them using the bread lame, making three cuts in each (see technique p. 54). Slide the baguettes, still on the parchment paper, onto the hot baking sheet or baking stone in the center of the oven and carefully pour the simmering water into the rimmed sheet on the lower rack to create steam. Quickly close the oven door and bake for 20 minutes. Immediately transfer the baguettes to a rack and let them cool completely at room temperature.

COUNTRY BREAD

Pain de campagne

Makes 3 loaves, weighing 10½ oz. (300 g) each

Active time

1½ hours

Bulk fermentation time

1½ hours

Resting time

30 minutes

Proofing time

1 hour

Cooking time

30 minutes

Storage

Up to 2 days wrapped in a clean dish towel

Equipment

Stand mixer + dough hook

Instant-read thermometer

Baker's couche (optional)

Heavy-duty baking sheet or baking stone

Bread lame

Ingredients

Scant 3½ cups (15 oz./425 g) white bread flour (T65)

Scant ¾ cup (2.5 oz./75 g) rye flour

1⅓ cups (315 g/315 ml) water

1¾ tsp (9 g) salt

0.1 oz. (2 g) fresh yeast

2.5 oz. (75 g) ripe liquid levain (see technique p. 40)

5 tsp (25 g/25 ml) water (for *bassinage*)

PREPARING THE DOUGH

Knead all the ingredients, except the 5 tsp (25 g/25 ml) water, in the bowl of the stand mixer on low speed for 5 minutes until well combined. Continue kneading on low speed until the gluten network begins to strengthen and the dough can be stretched easily but tears if stretched too far (about 3 minutes). With the mixer running on low speed, gradually add the 5 tsp (25 g/25 ml) water as needed, depending on the consistency of the dough (*bassinage*): the dough should be soft and supple but not too runny. Make sure the dough temperature does not exceed 73°F–75°F (23°C–24°C). Cover the bowl with plastic wrap and let the dough ferment for 1½ hours at room temperature, folding it once after 30 minutes (see technique p. 48). Divide the dough into 3 pieces weighing 10½ oz. (300 g) each, and gently shape each one into a ball. Let rest for 30 minutes in the refrigerator.

SHAPING AND PROOFING THE DOUGH

Shape each piece of dough into a *bâtard* (see Chefs' Notes p. 51) and place seam side up on a floured baker's couche or thick dish towel. Let proof for 1 hour at room temperature, covered with plastic wrap or a clean dish towel.

BAKING THE LOAVES

Place a heavy-duty baking sheet or baking stone on a rack in the center of the oven and an empty heavy-duty rimmed baking sheet on the bottom rack. Preheat the oven to 480°F (250°C/Gas Mark 9) and bring 1 cup (250 ml) water to a simmer. Invert the loaves onto a sheet of parchment paper and, using the bread lame, score them down the center, then score a chevon pattern on either side (see technique p. 56). Slide the loaves, still on the parchment paper, onto the hot baking sheet or baking stone in the center of the oven and carefully pour the simmering water into the rimmed sheet on the lower rack to create steam. Quickly close the oven door and bake for about 25 minutes, or until deeply golden. To thoroughly dry out the crust, lower the oven temperature to 400°F (200°C/Gas Mark 6). Open the door to release any steam, then close it again and let the bread dry for 5–10 minutes. The loaves should make a hollow sound when tapped on the bottom and the crust should be thick and crisp. Immediately transfer the loaves to a rack and let them cool completely at room temperature.

WHOLE WHEAT BREAD

Pain complet

Makes 3 loaves, weighing about 11.25 oz. (320 g) each

Active time
1½ hours

Autolyse time
30 minutes

Bulk fermentation time
30 minutes

Resting time
30 minutes

Proofing time
10–12 hours in the refrigerator

Cooking time
30–40 minutes

Storage
Up to 2 days wrapped in a clean dish towel

Equipment
Stand mixer + dough hook
Instant-read thermometer
3 loaf pans, 3 × 7 in. (7 × 18 cm), 3 in. (8 cm) deep
Bread lame

Ingredients
Scant 4½ cups (1 lb. 2 oz./500 g) whole wheat flour (T150)
1½ cups (340 g/340 ml) water
2½ tsp (13 g) salt
0.25 oz. (5 g) fresh yeast
3.5 oz. (100 g) ripe liquid levain (see technique p. 40)

PREPARING THE DOUGH (1 DAY AHEAD)
Knead all the ingredients, except the levain, in the bowl of the stand mixer on low speed for 3 minutes until well combined. Cover the bowl with plastic wrap and let rest for 30 minutes at room temperature (autolyse). Add the levain and knead on low speed for 10 minutes until combined. Increase the speed to high and knead for 4 minutes until the dough is supple. Make sure the dough temperature does not exceed 75°F (24°C). Place in a clean bowl, cover with plastic wrap, and let ferment for 30 minutes at room temperature. Divide the dough into 3 pieces weighing 11.25 oz. (320 g) each, and let rest for 30 minutes in the refrigerator.

SHAPING AND PROOFING THE DOUGH (1 DAY AHEAD)
Shape each piece of dough into a *bâtard* measuring 7 in. (18 cm) in length (see Chefs' Notes p. 51). Place in the loaf pans with the seams facing down and dust the tops with flour. Using the bread lame, score the tops with diagonal slashes (see technique p. 57). Cover loosely in plastic bags and let ferment for 10–12 hours in the refrigerator.

BAKING THE BREAD
The next day, remove the dough from the refrigerator 30 minutes before baking. Place a rack in the center of the oven and another rack directly below it. Place a heavy-duty rimmed baking sheet on the bottom rack and preheat the oven to 475°F (240°C/Gas Mark 9). Bring 1 cup (250 ml) water to a simmer. Place the loaves in the oven and carefully pour the simmering water into the rimmed sheet on the lower rack to create steam. Quickly close the oven door and bake the loaves for 30–40 minutes. Immediately turn the loaves out of the pans and let them cool completely on a rack.

RYE BREAD

Pain de seigle

Makes 3 loaves, weighing about 11.75 oz. (335 g) each

Active time

1½ hours

Bulk fermentation time

30 minutes

Resting time

30 minutes in the refrigerator

Proofing time

1 hour

Cooking time

30–40 minutes

Storage

Up to 2 days wrapped in a clean dish towel

Equipment

Stand mixer + dough hook

Instant-read thermometer

3 loaf pans, 3 × 7 in. (7 × 18 cm), 3 in. (8 cm) deep

Ingredients

3¾ cups (14 oz./400 g) rye flour (T130)

¾ cup + 2 tbsp (3.5 oz./100 g) white bread flour (T65)

1½ cups (340 g/340 ml) water

2 tsp (11 g) salt

0.25 oz. (5 g) fresh yeast

5.25 oz. (150 g) ripe stiff levain (see technique p. 38)

PREPARING THE DOUGH

Knead all the ingredients in the bowl of the stand mixer on low speed for 8 minutes until well combined. Increase the speed to medium and knead for 2 minutes. Make sure the dough temperature does not exceed 75°F (24°C). Cover with plastic wrap and let ferment for 30 minutes at room temperature. Divide the dough into 3 pieces weighing 11.75 oz. (335 g) each, shape each one into a ball, and let rest for 30 minutes in the refrigerator.

SHAPING AND PROOFING THE DOUGH

Shape each piece of dough into a *bâtard* measuring 7 in. (18 cm) in length (see Chefs' Notes p. 51). Place in the loaf pans with the seams facing up and dust the tops with flour. Let proof in a steam oven set to 75°F (24°C), or place on a rack in a turned-off oven above a bowl of boiling water, for 1 hour.

BAKING THE LOAVES

Place a rack in the center of the oven and another rack directly below it. Place a heavy-duty rimmed baking sheet on the bottom rack and preheat the oven to 450°F (240°C/Gas Mark 8). Bring 1 cup (250 ml) water to a simmer. Place the loaves in the oven and carefully pour the simmering water into the rimmed sheet on the lower rack to create steam. Quickly close the oven door and bake the loaves for 30–40 minutes, until golden. Immediately turn the loaves out of the pans and let them cool completely on a rack.

WHITE SOURDOUGH BREAD

Pain blanc sur levain liquide

Makes 2 loaves, weighing about 1 lb. 2 oz. (500 g) each

Active time

1½ hours

Autolyse time

30 minutes

Bulk fermentation time

2 hours

Resting time

30 minutes

Proofing time

2 hours at room temperature, or overnight in the refrigerator

Cooking time

20–25 minutes

Storage

Up to 2 days wrapped in a clean dish towel

Equipment

Stand mixer + dough hook

Instant-read thermometer

2 × 8-in. (20-cm) round bannetons (optional), floured

Heavy-duty baking sheet or baking stone

Bread lame

Ingredients

4 cups + 2 tbsp (1 lb. 2 oz./500 g) white bread flour (T65)

1⅓ cups (320 g/320 ml) water

3.5 oz. (100 g) young liquid levain (see technique p. 40)

2 tsp (11 g) salt

PREPARING THE DOUGH (1 DAY AHEAD IF PROOFING OVERNIGHT)

Knead the flour and water in the bowl of the stand mixer on low speed for 3 minutes until no dry bits remain. Cover the bowl with plastic wrap or a dish towel and let rest for 30 minutes at room temperature (autolyse). With the mixer running on low speed, add the levain in two equal quantities, followed by the salt. Knead on low speed for 8 minutes until well combined. Increase the speed to medium and knead for 2 minutes until the dough is supple and smooth. Make sure the dough temperature does not exceed 73°F–77°F (23°C–25°C). Cover the bowl with plastic wrap and let the dough ferment for 20 minutes at room temperature. Perform one fold (see technique p. 48), let the dough ferment for another 20 minutes, then make a second fold. Perform the third and final fold 20 minutes later. Let the dough ferment undisturbed for an additional 1 hour at room temperature. Divide the dough into 2 pieces weighing about 1 lb. 2 oz. (500 g) each. Flatten slightly and fold the four corners of each piece in toward the center, turn them over, and gently shape into balls between your hands. Let rest for 30 minutes at room temperature.

SHAPING AND PROOFING THE DOUGH (1 DAY AHEAD IF PROOFING OVERNIGHT)

Flatten the balls of dough to burst any air bubbles, then gently reshape each piece of dough into a loose boule (see technique p. 50). Place the boules seam side up on a floured thick dish towel, or in the bannetons if using. Let proof for 2 hours at room temperature, or overnight in the refrigerator. For the overnight option, cover with plastic wrap or place the bannetons in loose-fitting plastic bags and seal shut.

BAKING THE LOAVES

Place a heavy-duty baking sheet or baking stone on a rack in the center of the oven and an empty heavy-duty rimmed baking sheet on the bottom rack. Preheat the oven to 450°F (240°C/Gas Mark 8) and bring 1 cup (250 ml) water to a simmer. Invert the boules onto a sheet of parchment paper and score the dough with a zigzag or cross pattern (see technique p. 55). Slide the parchment paper onto the hot baking sheet in the center of the oven and carefully pour the simmering water into the rimmed sheet on the lower rack to create steam. Quickly close the oven door and bake for 20–25 minutes, until golden brown. To thoroughly dry out the crust, lower the oven temperature to 400°F (200°C/Gas Mark 6). Open the door once or twice to release any steam, then close it again and let the bread dry for 5–10 minutes. Alternatively, if the bread is already deeply browned, do this step in a turned-off oven. The bread should make a hollow sound when tapped on the bottom, and the crust should be thick and crisp. Immediately transfer the loaves to a rack and let them cool completely at room temperature.

VIENNA BAGUETTES

Baguette viennoise

Makes 6 small baguettes, weighing about 6 oz. (165 g) each

Active time
1½ hours

***Pâte fermentée* fermentation time**
Overnight

Bulk fermentation time
45 minutes–1 hour

Resting time
15 minutes

Proofing time
1¼–1½ hours

Cooking time
12–15 minutes

Storage
Up to 2 days wrapped in a clean dish towel

Equipment
Stand mixer + dough hook
Instant-read thermometer
Baguette pans for 6 half-baguettes
Bread lame

Ingredients

Pâte fermentée
½ cup minus 1 tbsp (1.75 oz./50 g) white bread flour (T65)
2 tbsp (30 g/30 ml) water
0.05 oz. (1 g) salt
0.05 oz. (1 g) fresh yeast

Vienna bread dough
3¼ cups (14 oz./400 g) white bread flour (T65)
¾ cup + 2 tbsp (3.5 oz./100 g) all-purpose flour (*gruau*)
1 egg
Scant 1 cup (230 g/230 ml) water
¼ cup (25 g) milk powder
2½ tbsp (1 oz./30 g) sugar
1 oz. (25 g) fresh yeast
2 tsp (10 g) salt
2.75 oz. (80 g) *pâte fermentée* (see above)
3 tbsp (1.5 oz./40 g) butter, diced, at room temperature

Egg wash
1 egg
1 egg yolk
2 tsp (10 g/10 ml) whole milk

PREPARING THE PÂTE FERMENTÉE (1 DAY AHEAD)
Mix the flour, water, salt, and yeast together in the bowl of the stand mixer and knead on low speed, or by hand, for 10 minutes, until smooth. Place in a bowl, cover with plastic wrap, and let ferment overnight in the refrigerator.

PREPARING THE VIENNA BREAD DOUGH
Knead all the dough ingredients, except the butter, in the bowl of the stand mixer on low speed for 4 minutes until well combined. Increase the speed to high and knead for 4 minutes until the dough is supple and elastic. With the mixer running on low speed, add the butter and knead until completely incorporated (6–8 minutes). Make sure the dough temperature does not exceed 75°F (24°C). Transfer to a clean bowl, cover with plastic wrap, and let ferment for 45 minutes–1 hour at room temperature.

SHAPING AND PROOFING THE DOUGH
Divide the dough into 6 pieces weighing about 6 oz. (165 g) each. Shape into small baguettes (see technique p. 51) and place in the baguette pans. Let rest for 15 minutes. Whisk together the egg wash ingredients and brush over the baguettes. Using the bread lame, score with diagonal slashes (see technique p. 57). Let proof in a steam oven set to 75°F (24°C), or place on a rack in a turned-off oven above a bowl of boiling water, for 1¼–1½ hours.

BAKING THE BAGUETTES
Preheat the oven to 425°F (220°C/Gas Mark 7). Brush the baguettes again with egg wash and bake for 12–15 minutes. Immediately remove the baguettes from the pans. Place on a rack and let cool at room temperature.

SANDWICH BREAD

Pain de mie

Makes 3 loaves, weighing about 12 oz. (330 g) each

Active time
1½ hours

***Pâte fermentée* fermentation time**
Overnight

Bulk fermentation time
45 minutes

Resting time
15 minutes

Proofing time
1¼–1½ hours

Cooking time
25–30 minutes

Storage
Up to several days in a well-sealed plastic bag

Equipment
Stand mixer + dough hook
Instant-read thermometer
3 Pullman (*pain de mie*) loaf pans, 3 × 7 in. (8 × 18 cm), 3 in. (8 cm) deep

Ingredients

Pâte fermentée
½ cup + 1 tbsp (2.5 oz./70 g) white bread flour (T65)
3 tbsp (43 g/43 ml) water
0.05 oz. (1 g) salt
0.05 oz. (1 g) fresh yeast

Sandwich bread dough
4 cups + 2 tbsp (1 lb. 2 oz./500 g) white bread flour (T65)
1 cup (250 g/250 ml) water
Scant ¼ cup (25 g) milk powder
2 tbsp (25 g) sugar
1 oz. (25 g) fresh yeast
2 tsp (10 g) salt
4 oz. (115 g) *pâte fermentée* (see above)
3 tbsp (1.75 oz./50 g) butter, diced, at room temperature

Butter for the pans

PREPARING THE PÂTE FERMENTÉE (1 DAY AHEAD)
Mix the flour, water, salt, and yeast together in the bowl of the stand mixer and knead on low speed, or by hand, for 10 minutes, until smooth. Place in a bowl, cover with plastic wrap, and let ferment overnight in the refrigerator.

PREPARING THE DOUGH
Knead all the ingredients in the bowl of the stand mixer on low speed for 3 minutes until well combined. Increase the speed to high and knead for 7 minutes until the dough is supple and elastic. Make sure the dough temperature does not exceed 75°F (24°C). Place the dough in a clean bowl, cover with plastic wrap, and let ferment for 45 minutes at room temperature. Divide the dough into 3 pieces weighing about 12 oz. (330 g) each, and gently shape each one into a ball. Let rest for 15 minutes at room temperature.

SHAPING AND PROOFING THE DOUGH
Grease the bases and lids of the loaf pans with butter. Shape the dough into *bâtards* measuring 6 in. (15 cm) in length (see Chefs' Notes p. 51). Place in the pans and cover with the lids. Let proof in a steam oven set to 75°F (24°C), or on a rack in a turned-off oven above a bowl of boiling water, for 1¼–1½ hours.

BAKING THE LOAVES
Preheat the oven to 425°F (220°C/Gas Mark 7) and bake the loaves for 25–30 minutes. Immediately turn them out of the pans onto a rack and let cool completely at room temperature.

SPECIALTY BREADS

RICE AND BUCKWHEAT ROLLS

Pain au levain de riz et sarrasin

Makes 10 rolls, weighing about 3.5 oz. (100 g) each

Active time

1½ hours

Fermentation time (for levain)

About 5 hours

Proofing time

20–40 minutes

Cooking time

40–45 minutes

Storage

Up to several days in an airtight container

Equipment

Stand mixer + paddle beater

Instant-read thermometer

10 oval-shaped pans, 3 × 5 in. (8 × 12 cm), 1½ in. (4 cm) deep

Dough scraper

Heavy-duty baking sheet or baking stone

Ingredients

Buckwheat and rice levain

2 oz. (60 g) ripe liquid *levain-chef* (see techniques pp. 36 and 40 and Chefs' Notes)

⅓ cup (80 g/80 ml) water at 113°F (45°C)

½ cup (2.25 oz./65 g) buckwheat flour

Scant ½ cup (2.25 oz./65 g) rice flour

Batter

7 oz. (200 g) ripe buckwheat and rice levain (see above)

0.25 oz. (7 g) fresh yeast

2½ cups (12.5 oz./350 g) rice flour

1 cup + 2 tbsp (5.25 oz./150 g) buckwheat flour

2 tsp (10 g) salt

Scant 1½ cups (350 g/350 ml) water

Butter or neutral oil for the pans

Topping

Generous ½ cup (3.5 oz./100 g) kasha (roasted buckwheat groats)

PREPARING THE BUCKWHEAT AND RICE LEVAIN

Using the ingredients listed, follow the technique for liquid levain (see technique p. 40). Let ferment for about 5 hours, or until ripe (*tout point*).

PREPARING THE BATTER

In the stand mixer fitted with the paddle beater (as the batter will be quite liquid), beat all the ingredients for 5 minutes on low speed until well combined. The mixture should have the consistency of a crêpe batter. Ensure the temperature of the batter does not exceed 86°F (30°C).

PROOFING THE BATTER

Grease the pans with butter or neutral oil and fill each one with 3.5 oz. (100 g) batter. Wet the dough scraper with water and use to smooth over the tops. Scatter the kasha over half of each roll. Let proof for 20–40 minutes in a steam oven set to 86°F (30°C), or on a rack in a turned-off oven above a bowl of boiling water, until cracks form on the surface.

BAKING THE ROLLS

Place a heavy-duty baking sheet or baking stone on a rack in the center of the oven and an empty heavy-duty rimmed baking sheet on the bottom rack. Preheat the oven to 450°F (230°C/Gas Mark 8) and bring 1 cup (250 ml) water to a simmer. Place the pans on the hot baking sheet and carefully pour the simmering water into the rimmed sheet on the lower rack to create steam. Quickly close the oven door and bake for 20–25 minutes, then lower the oven temperature to 410°F (210°C/Gas Mark 6) and continue to bake for about 20 minutes to dry the rolls out a little. Immediately turn the rolls out of the pans and let them cool completely on a rack.

CHEFS' NOTES

This recipe is relatively low in gluten, but if you'd like to make it 100 percent gluten free, prepare a *levain-chef* using gluten-free flours.

INJERA (GLUTEN-FREE)

Makes 8 large (or 16 small) injeras

Active time

1½ hours

Fermentation time

24–48 hours (*levain-chef*) + overnight, or up to 3 days (refreshing levain)

Bulk fermentation time

2–3 hours + 2 hours

Proofing time

2 hours

Cooking time

1–2 minutes per injera

Storage

Up to several days in the refrigerator, rolled up in plastic wrap

Equipment

Large glass or other non-reactive container

Bowl scraper

Stand mixer + paddle beater

Instant-read thermometer

8-in. (20-cm) skillet

Ingredients

Gluten-free *levain-chef*

¾ tsp (5 g) honey

Scant ½ cup (100 g/100 ml) water at 113°F (45°C)

3 oz. (85 g) teff flour

Refreshed gluten-free levain

1 cup (250 g/250 ml) water at 113°F (45°C)

1.75 oz. (50 g) liquid gluten-free *levain-chef* (see above)

Scant 2 cups (9 oz./250 g) teff flour

Injera batter

1 cup (250 g/250 ml) water at 113°F (45°C)

Scant 2 cups (9 oz./250 g) teff flour

Refreshed gluten-free levain (see above)

Neutral oil for the pan

PREPARING THE GLUTEN-FREE LEVAIN-CHEF (3–5 DAYS AHEAD)

In a large glass or other non-reactive container, make the gluten-free *levain-chef* using the ingredients listed (see technique p. 36).

PREPARING THE REFRESHED GLUTEN-FREE LEVAIN (1–3 DAYS AHEAD)

In a large glass or other non-reactive container, refresh the gluten-free *levain-chef* using the ingredients listed (see technique p. 40). Let ferment in a steam oven set between 86°F–95°F (30°C–35°C), or place on a rack in a turned-off oven above a bowl of boiling water, for 2–3 hours. The levain should expand and begin to crack on the surface. Cover with plastic wrap and let ferment in the refrigerator, at least overnight and up to 3 days.

PREPARING THE INJERA BATTER

The next day, beat the water, teff flour, and refreshed levain in the bowl of the stand mixer for 5 minutes on low speed. Make sure the batter temperature does not exceed 68°F (20°C). Place a bowl of boiling water in a warm oven (95°F/35°C) and place the batter above it. Let ferment for 2 hours until the surface is bubbly.

COOKING THE INJERAS

Lightly grease an 8-in. (20-cm) skillet with a little oil and warm over high heat. When the skillet is hot, pour in a little injera batter to coat the skillet: injeras should be about ¼ in. (6 mm) thick (a little thicker than crêpes, but not quite as thick as pancakes). Cover the skillet and cook on one side only for 1–2 minutes until set. Using a large spatula, carefully remove the injera from the pan and place between two clean dish towels to keep it moist. Repeat with the remaining batter.

CHEFS' NOTES

In East Africa, injera serves as an eating utensil; it is used to scoop food off the plate. This bread has a very sour taste, so feel free to add a little sugar when serving to temper the tangy flavor.

CHESTNUT BREAD ROLLS (GLUTEN-FREE)

Pain à la châtaigne

Makes 10 individual rolls, weighing about 3.5 oz. (100 g) each

Active time
1½ hours

Resting time
10 minutes

Proofing time
1½ –2 hours

Cooking time
35 minutes

Storage
Up to 2 days in an airtight container

Equipment
Stand mixer + paddle beater
Instant-read thermometer

Ingredients
1¾ cups (450 g/450 ml) water
2 tbsp (1.5 oz./40 g) honey
2½ tbsp (40 g/40 ml) apple cider vinegar
Scant 3 tbsp (1.5 oz./40 g) psyllium husk powder
1 cup (3.5 oz./100 g) chestnut flour
2 tsp (8 g) baking powder
1½ tsp (8 g) salt
1¼ cups (3.5 oz./100 g) rolled oats
Scant ¾ cup (3.5 oz./100 g) flax seeds
Scant ¾ cup (3.5 oz./100 g) sunflower seeds
0.35 oz. (10 g) fresh yeast, crumbled
Generous 2 tbsp (30 g/35 ml) neutral vegetable oil

PREPARING THE DOUGH
Whisk together the water, honey, vinegar, and psyllium husk powder in a bowl. Let rest for 10 minutes. The mixture should have a gel-like consistency. Mix together the chestnut flour, baking powder, salt, oats, and seeds in the bowl of the stand mixer, then add the psyllium husk mixture and remaining ingredients. Mix on low speed until the dough pulls away from the sides of the bowl (it will still be a little sticky). Make sure the dough temperature does not exceed 86°F (30°C).

SHAPING AND PROOFING THE DOUGH
Divide the dough into 10 pieces weighing 2.75–3.5 oz. (80–100 g) each and shape into individual rolls. Set on a baking sheet lined with parchment paper. Let proof in a steam oven set to 75°F (24°C), or place on a rack in a turned-off oven above a bowl of boiling water, for 1½ –2 hours. The dough should collapse slightly.

BAKING THE ROLLS
Place a rack in the center of the oven and another rack directly below it. Place a heavy-duty rimmed baking sheet on the bottom rack and preheat the oven to 375°F (190°C/Gas Mark 5). Bring 1 cup (250 ml) water to a simmer. Place the rolls on the baking sheet in the oven and carefully pour the simmering water into the rimmed sheet on the lower rack to create steam. Quickly close the oven door and bake the rolls for about 35 minutes. Transfer the rolls to a rack and let them cool at room temperature.

CHEFS' NOTES

- Psyllium husk powder gives the dough a somewhat gelatinous texture, and the resulting bread is soft with a tender crust.
- To boost the flavor of the flax and sunflower seeds, lightly toast them in the oven at 325°F (160°C/Gas Mark 3) for about 20 minutes before adding them to the dough.

STONEGROUND WHEAT LOAVES

Pain nutrition au levain

Makes 2 loaves, weighing 15 oz. (425 g) each

Active time

2 hours

Bulk fermentation time

2 hours + overnight

Resting time

30 minutes

Proofing time

1 hour

Cooking time

30–40 minutes

Storage

Up to 3 days rolled up in a clean dish towel

Equipment

Instant-read thermometer

Baker's couche (optional)

Heavy-duty baking sheet or baking stone

Rosette stencil

Bread lame

Ingredients

Dough

Scant 1½ cups (350 g/350 ml) water

Scant 1½ tsp (7 g) salt

0.25 oz. (5 g) ripe liquid levain (see technique p. 40)

Scant 4½ cups (1 lb. 2 oz./500 g) stoneground white whole wheat flour (T80)

Decoration

Flour

PREPARING THE DOUGH (1 DAY AHEAD)

Whisk together the water and salt in a large bowl until the salt dissolves, then whisk in the levain until diluted. Add the flour and mix it in using your fingertips until well combined (see technique p. 46, steps 1 and 2). The dough will be sticky. Make sure the dough temperature does not exceed 75°F–77°F (24°C–25°C). Place the dough in a clean bowl, cover with plastic wrap, and let ferment for 2 hours at room temperature, folding it every 30 minutes for a total of 4 folds (see technique p. 48). After the fourth fold, cover the bowl and let the dough ferment overnight at room temperature.

SHAPING AND PROOFING THE DOUGH

The next day, divide the dough into 2 pieces weighing 15 oz. (425 g) each. Shape into balls and let rest for 30 minutes at room temperature. Shape into baguettes with slightly pointed tips (see technique p. 51). Place them seam side down on a floured baker's couche or clean heavy dish towel. Pleat the couche or dish towel like an accordion between them to maintain their shape and let proof for 1 hour at room temperature in a draft-free place.

SCORING AND BAKING THE LOAVES

Place a heavy-duty baking sheet or baking stone on a rack in the center of the oven and a heavy-duty rimmed baking sheet on the bottom rack. Preheat the oven to 500°F (260°C/Gas Mark 10). Bring 1 cup (250 ml) water to a simmer. Invert the loaves onto parchment paper, place the rosace stencil over them, and dust with a very thin layer of flour. Using the bread lame, score lengthwise down the center of each one. Slide the parchment paper onto the hot baking sheet in the center of the oven and carefully pour the simmering water into the rimmed sheet on the lower rack to create steam. Quickly close the oven door and bake for 25 minutes. Once the crust is golden, lower the oven temperature to 350°F (180°C/Gas Mark 4), open the door to release any steam, and then close it again. Continue to bake for an additional 5–10 minutes to dry out the crust. Immediately transfer the loaves to a rack and let them cool completely at room temperature.

MULTISEED WHOLEGRAIN ROLLS

Pain nutrition aux graines

Makes 10 rolls, weighing 3.75 oz. (110 g) each

Active time
2 hours

Pre-ferment fermentation time
Overnight

Bulk fermentation time
4 hours

Resting time
30 minutes

Proofing time
1 hour

Cooking time
20 minutes

Storage
Up to 2 days wrapped in a clean dish towel

Equipment
Blender
Instant-read thermometer

Ingredients

Pre-ferment

- Scant 3 tbsp (25 g) hulled hemp seeds
- Generous 1 tbsp (25 g) amaranth grain
- Scant 2 tbsp (25 g) nigella seeds
- ½ cup (125 g/125 ml) water at 95°F (35°C)
- 0.35 oz. (10 g) ripe liquid levain (see technique p. 40)

Dough

- Scant 1½ cups (350 g/350 ml) water
- 2 tsp (10 g) salt
- 0.05 oz. (1 g) fresh yeast
- Pre-ferment (see above)
- Scant 4½ cups (1 lb. 2 oz./500 g) stoneground white whole wheat flour (T80)

To assemble

- Poppy seeds
- Olive oil

PREPARING THE PRE-FERMENT (1 DAY AHEAD)
Place all the seeds together in the blender and pulse to lightly crush them, without grinding them to a powder. Add the water and levain. Blend until well combined, transfer to a bowl, and cover with plastic wrap. Let ferment overnight in the refrigerator.

PREPARING THE DOUGH
The next day, whisk together the water and salt in a large bowl until the salt dissolves, then whisk in the yeast and pre-ferment until well blended. Add the flour and mix it in using your fingertips until well combined (see technique p. 46, steps 1 and 2). The dough will be sticky. Make sure the dough temperature does not exceed 75°F–77°F (24°C–25°C). Cover the bowl with plastic wrap and let the dough ferment for a total of 2½ hours at room temperature, performing 5 folds during this time (see technique p. 48): fold the dough 3 times every ten minutes, let ferment for 30 minutes before folding it again, then let ferment for an additional 30 minutes before performing the 5th and final fold. Let the dough ferment undisturbed for an additional 1 hour at room temperature. Divide the dough into 20 pieces: 10 weighing 3.25 oz. (90 g) each (the bases) and 10 weighing about 0.75 oz. (20 g) each (the tops). Gently shape into balls and let rest for 30 minutes at room temperature.

ASSEMBLING AND PROOFING THE ROLLS
Shape the larger dough pieces into taut balls (see technique p. 50) and roll the smaller pieces into disks with a slightly smaller diameter than the balls. Moisten the tops of the disks with a little water and dip them into poppy seeds to coat. Place seed side down on a clean dish towel and brush around the edges with a little olive oil. Set on top of the bases with the seeds facing up and press down gently to seal well. Place the rolls seed side down on a baking sheet lined with parchment paper. Let proof in a steam oven set to 75°F (24°C), or on a rack in a turned-off oven above a bowl of boiling water, for 1 hour.

BAKING THE ROLLS
Place a rack in the center of the oven and another rack directly below it. Place a heavy-duty rimmed baking sheet on the bottom rack and preheat the oven to 500°F (260°C/Gas Mark 10). Bring 1 cup (250 ml) water to a simmer. Delicately turn the rolls over on the parchment paper, so the seeds are facing up, and place the rolls on the baking sheet in the oven. Carefully pour the simmering water into the rimmed sheet on the lower rack to create steam. Quickly close the oven door and bake for 20 minutes. Immediately transfer the rolls to a rack and let them cool completely at room temperature.

CHEFS' NOTES

Soaking the seeds during the pre-ferment fermentation is important to break them down and make them easier to digest.

FRUIT AND NUT LOAF

Pavé aux fruits

Makes 1 loaf, weighing about 2¼ lb. (1 kg)

Active time

1½ hours

Bulk fermentation time

1½ hours

Resting time

30 minutes

Proofing time

12–16 hours

Cooking time

40–45 minutes

Storage

Up to 2 days wrapped in a clean dish towel

Equipment

Stand mixer + dough hook

Instant-read thermometer

Bread lame

Heavy-duty baking sheet or baking stone

Ingredients

2¾ cups (12.5 oz./350 g) white bread flour (T65)

1 cup + 2 tbsp (5.25 oz./150 g) white whole wheat flour (T80)

1½ cups (375 g/375 ml) water

Scant 2½ tsp (12 g) salt

0.1 oz. (2 g) fresh yeast

3.5 oz. (100 g) ripe stiff levain (see technique p. 38)

1 cup (5.25 oz./150 g) hazelnuts, chopped

1¼ cups (5.25 oz./150 g) dried cranberries

1 cup (5.25 oz./150 g) dried apricots

3½ tbsp (50 g/50 ml) water (for *bassinage*)

Extra flour, for dusting

PREPARING THE DOUGH (1 DAY AHEAD)

Knead all the ingredients, except the hazelnuts, dried fruits, and 3½ tbsp (50 g/50 ml) water, in the bowl of the stand mixer on low speed for 3 minutes, until well combined. Increase the speed to medium and knead for 6 minutes until the dough is supple and smooth. Add the hazelnuts and dried fruit, and knead for 1–2 minutes until evenly distributed. Gradually incorporate the 3½ tbsp (50 g/50 ml) water as needed, depending on the consistency of the dough, which should be supple (*bassinage*). Make sure the dough temperature does not exceed 77°F (25°C). Place in a clean bowl, cover with plastic wrap, and let ferment for 45 minutes at room temperature. Give the dough one fold (see technique p. 48), cover again with plastic wrap, and let ferment for an additional 45 minutes. Perform a second fold, then shape the dough into a ball, return it to the bowl, and cover with plastic wrap. Let rest for 30 minutes in the refrigerator.

SHAPING AND PROOFING THE DOUGH (1 DAY AHEAD)

Flatten the dough slightly and fold the four corners in toward the center, turn it over, and shape it into a 10 × 16-in. (25 × 40-cm) loaf. Place on a clean dish towel, cover loosely with plastic wrap or a dish towel, and let proof for 12–16 hours in the refrigerator.

BAKING THE LOAF

The next day, place a heavy-duty baking sheet or baking stone on a rack in the center of the oven and an empty heavy-duty rimmed baking sheet on the bottom rack. Preheat the oven to 480°F (250°C/Gas Mark 10) and bring 1 cup (250 ml) water to a simmer. Invert the dough onto parchment paper. Dust it evenly with flour and, using the bread lame, score the top with a crosshatch cut (see technique p. 58). Slide the parchment paper onto the hot baking sheet or baking stone in the center of the oven and carefully pour the simmering water into the rimmed sheet on the lower rack to create steam. Quickly close the oven door, lower the oven temperature to 450°F (230°C/Gas Mark 8), and bake for 40–45 minutes. Immediately transfer the loaf to a rack and let cool completely at room temperature.

FIG BREAD

Pain aux figues

Makes 3 loaves, weighing about 14 oz. (400 g) each

Active time

1½ hours

***Pâte fermentée* fermentation time**

Overnight

Bulk fermentation time

1 hour + 10–12 hours in the refrigerator

Proofing time

45 minutes

Cooking time

30–40 minutes

Storage

Up to 2 days wrapped in a clean dish towel

Equipment

Stand mixer + dough hook

Instant-read thermometer

3 bannetons, 6 × 7½ in. (15 × 19 cm), 1½ in. (4 cm) deep

Bread lame

Ingredients

Pâte fermentée

1 cup (4 oz./120 g) white bread flour (T65)

⅓ cup (75 g/75 ml) water

¼ tsp (2 g) salt

0.1 oz. (2 g) fresh yeast

Dough

3¼ cups (14 oz./400 g) white bread flour (T65)

Scant ½ cup (1.75 oz./50 g) whole wheat flour (T150)

Scant ½ cup (1.75 oz./50 g) rye flour

1½ cups (340 g/340 ml) water

1 tsp (5 g) salt

0.35 oz. (10 g) fresh yeast

7 oz. (200 g) *pâte fermentée* (see above)

5.25 oz. (150 g) dried figs, chopped

PREPARING THE PÂTE FERMENTÉE (2 DAYS AHEAD)

Mix the flour, water, salt, and yeast together in the bowl of the stand mixer and knead on low speed, or by hand, for 10 minutes, until smooth. Place in a bowl, cover with plastic wrap, and let ferment overnight in the refrigerator.

PREPARING THE DOUGH (1 DAY AHEAD)

The next day, knead all the ingredients, except the figs, in the bowl of the stand mixer on low speed for 5 minutes until well combined. Increase the speed to medium and knead for 4 minutes. With the mixer running on low speed, add the figs and continue to knead for an additional 4 minutes until well distributed. Make sure the dough temperature does not exceed 75°F (24°C). Place the dough in a clean bowl, cover with plastic wrap, and let ferment for 1 hour at room temperature. Fold the dough once halfway through the fermentation time, after 30 minutes (see technique p. 48). Let ferment for 10–12 hours in the refrigerator, covered with plastic wrap.

SHAPING AND PROOFING THE DOUGH

The next day, flour the bannetons and divide the dough into 3 pieces weighing 14 oz. (400 g) each. Shape each one into a *bâtard* measuring 6 in. (15 cm) in length (see technique p. 51) and place in the bannetons. Let proof in a steam oven set to 75°F (24°C), or on a rack in a turned-off oven above a bowl of boiling water, for 45 minutes.

BAKING THE FIG BREAD

Place a rack in the center of the oven and another rack directly below it. Place a heavy-duty rimmed baking sheet on the bottom rack and preheat the oven to 480°F (250°C/Gas Mark 10). Bring 1 cup (250 ml) water to a simmer. Invert the bannetons onto a baking sheet lined with parchment paper and score each loaf with a crosshatch cut (see technique p. 58). Place the loaves on the baking sheet in the oven and carefully pour the simmering water into the rimmed sheet on the lower rack to create steam. Quickly close the oven door and bake for 30–40 minutes. Immediately transfer the loaves to a rack and let them cool completely at room temperature.

OLIVE BREAD

Pain aux olives

Makes 3 loaves, weighing about 14 oz. (400 g) each

Active time

1½ hours

***Pâte fermentée* fermentation time**

Overnight

Bulk fermentation time

1 hour + 10–12 hours in the refrigerator

Proofing time

45 minutes

Cooking time

30–40 minutes

Storage

Up to 2 days wrapped in a clean dish towel

Equipment

Stand mixer + dough hook

Instant-read thermometer

Bread lame

Ingredients

Pâte fermentée

1½ cups (6 oz./180 g) white bread flour (T65)

Scant ½ cup (112 g/112 ml) water

½ tsp (3 g) salt

0.2 oz. (3 g) fresh yeast

Olive mixture

1.75 oz. (50 g) pitted black olives, roughly chopped

1.75 oz. (50 g) pitted green olives, roughly chopped

0.25 oz. (5 g) basil leaves, chopped

Scant 2 tbsp (25 g/27 ml) extra virgin olive oil

Olive bread dough

4 cups + 2 tbsp (1 lb. 2 oz./500 g) white bread flour (T65)

1⅓ cups (325 g/325 ml) water

2 tsp (10 g) salt

0.25 oz. (5 g) fresh yeast

10½ oz. (300 g) *pâte fermentée* (see above)

Olive mixture (see above)

PREPARING THE PÂTE FERMENTÉE (2 DAYS AHEAD)

Mix the flour, water, salt, and yeast together in the bowl of the stand mixer and knead on low speed, or by hand, for 10 minutes until smooth. Place in a bowl, cover with plastic wrap, and let ferment overnight in the refrigerator.

PREPARING THE OLIVE MIXTURE (1 DAY AHEAD)

Combine all the olive mixture ingredients in a bowl.

PREPARING THE OLIVE BREAD DOUGH (1 DAY AHEAD)

Knead all the olive bread dough ingredients, except the olive mixture, in the bowl of the stand mixer on low speed for 5 minutes until well combined. Increase the speed to medium and knead for 6 minutes. With the mixer running on low speed, add the olive mixture and continue to knead for 2 minutes until well distributed. Make sure the dough temperature does not exceed 75°F (24°C). Place in a clean bowl, cover with plastic wrap, and let ferment for 30 minutes at room temperature. Fold the dough once, then cover with plastic wrap and let ferment for 10–12 hours in the refrigerator.

SHAPING AND PROOFING THE DOUGH

The next day, divide the dough into 3 pieces weighing 14 oz. (400 g) each. Shape each one into a *bâtard* measuring 8 in. (20 cm) in length (see technique p. 51) and place on a baking sheet lined with parchment paper. Let proof in a steam oven set to 75°F (24°C), or on a rack in a turned-off oven above a bowl of boiling water, for 45 minutes.

BAKING THE LOAVES

Place a rack in the center of the oven and another rack directly below it. Place a heavy-duty rimmed baking sheet on the bottom rack and preheat the oven to 480°F (250°C/Gas Mark 10). Bring 1 cup (250 ml) water to a simmer. Using the bread lame, score each loaf lengthwise down the center. Place the loaves on the baking sheet in the oven and carefully pour the simmering water into the rimmed sheet on the lower rack to create steam. Quickly close the oven door and bake for 30–40 minutes. Immediately transfer the loaves to a rack and let them cool completely at room temperature.

WALNUT BREAD

Pain aux noix

Makes 3 loaves, weighing about 13.5 oz. (385 g) each

Active time

1½ hours

Bulk fermentation time

30 minutes

Resting time

30 minutes in the refrigerator

Proofing time

1 hour

Cooking time

30–40 minutes

Storage time

Up to 3 days wrapped in a clean dish towel

Equipment

Stand mixer + dough hook

Instant-read thermometer

3 loaf pans, 3 × 7 in. (7 × 18 cm), 3 in. (8 cm) deep

Bread lame

Ingredients

3¾ cups (14 oz./400 g) rye flour

¾ cup + 2 tbsp (3.5 oz./100 g) white bread flour (T65), plus extra for dusting

1½ cups (340 g/340 ml) water

2 tsp (11 g) salt

0.25 oz. (5 g) fresh yeast

5.25 oz. (150 g) ripe stiff levain (see technique p. 38)

1¼ cups (5.25 oz./150 g) walnut halves

PREPARING THE DOUGH

Knead all the dough ingredients, except the walnut halves, in the bowl of the stand mixer on low speed for 8 minutes until well combined. Increase the speed to medium and knead for 2 minutes. With the mixer running on low speed, add the walnuts and continue to knead for an additional 2 minutes. Make sure the dough temperature does not exceed 75°F (24°C). Place in a clean bowl, cover with plastic wrap, and let ferment for 30 minutes at room temperature. Divide the dough into 3 pieces weighing 13.5 oz. (385 g) each, shape into balls, and let rest for 30 minutes in the refrigerator.

SHAPING AND PROOFING THE DOUGH

Shape each piece of dough into a *bâtard* measuring 7 in. (18 cm) in length (see technique p. 51). Place in the loaf pans with the seams facing down and dust the tops with flour. Using the bread lame, score the tops with diagonal slashes (see technique p. 57). Let proof in a steam oven set to 75°F (24°C), or place on a rack in a turned-off oven above a bowl of boiling water, for 1 hour.

BAKING THE LOAVES

Place a rack in the center of the oven and another rack directly below it. Place a heavy-duty rimmed baking sheet on the bottom rack and preheat the oven to 475°F (240°C/Gas Mark 9). Bring 1 cup (250 ml) water to a simmer. Place the loaves in the oven and carefully pour the simmering water into the rimmed sheet on the lower rack to create steam. Quickly close the oven door and bake the loaves for 30–40 minutes. Immediately turn the loaves out of the pans and let them cool completely on a rack.

BACON ROLLS

Pains aux lardons

Makes 9 rolls, weighing about 3.5 oz. (100 g) each

Active time

1½ hours

Autolyse time

30 minutes–1 hour

Bulk fermentation time

1 hour

Resting time

30 minutes

Proofing time

1 hour

Cooking time

14 minutes

Storage

Up to 24 hours wrapped in a clean dish towel

Equipment

Stand mixer + dough hook

Instant-read thermometer

Bread lame

Ingredients

Dough

2 cups (9 oz./250 g) white bread flour (T65)

2¼ cups (9 oz./250 g) white whole wheat flour (T80)

Scant 1½ cups (330 g/330 ml) water

3.5 oz. (100 g) ripe liquid levain (see technique p. 40)

0.25 oz. (5 g) fresh yeast

1¾ tsp (9 g) salt

Bacon topping

7 oz. (200 g) smoked bacon, thinly sliced crosswise (*lardons*)

PREPARING THE DOUGH

Knead the bread flour, whole wheat flour, and water in the bowl of the stand mixer on low speed for 5 minutes until no dry bits remain. Cover the bowl with a dish towel and let rest for 30 minutes–1 hour at room temperature (autolyse). Add the levain, yeast, and salt and knead on low speed for 5 minutes, then increase the speed to high and knead for 3 minutes until the dough is smooth. Make sure the dough temperature does not exceed 77°F (25°C). Place in a clean bowl, cover with plastic wrap, and let the dough ferment for 1 hour at room temperature, folding it once after 30 minutes (see technique p. 48). Divide the dough into 9 pieces weighing 3.5 oz. (100 g) each. Flatten each piece into an approximate 3 × 4-in. (8 × 10-cm) rectangle, then fold in half lengthwise to obtain 9 rectangles measuring 1½ × 4 in. (4 × 10 cm) each. Cover with plastic wrap and let rest for 30 minutes.

PREPARING THE BACON

To remove excess grease from the bacon, cook it in boiling water for a few minutes or fry it briefly in a hot skillet. Drain on paper towel and let cool.

SHAPING AND PROOFING THE ROLLS

Gently shape the pieces of dough into balls and scatter the lardons over the top. Shape into small baguettes (see technique p. 51) and place seam side down on a baking sheet lined with parchment paper. Let proof for 1 hour at room temperature in a draft-free place.

SCORING AND BAKING THE ROLLS

Place a rack in the center of the oven and another rack directly below it. Place a heavy-duty rimmed baking sheet on the bottom rack and preheat the oven to 500°F (260°C/Gas Mark 10). Bring 1 cup (250 ml) water to a simmer. Using the bread lame, score each roll lengthwise down the center—be sure to cut deeply enough to expose the bacon. Place in the oven and carefully pour the simmering water into the rimmed sheet on the lower rack to create steam. Quickly close the oven door and bake the rolls for 14 minutes. Take care not to overcook them to ensure they remain soft. Immediately transfer the rolls to a rack and let them cool slightly at room temperature. Serve warm with a good aperitif.

TURMERIC BREAD

Pain au curcuma

Makes 2 loaves, weighing about 13 oz. (370 g) each

Active time

1½ hours

Bulk fermentation time

1 hour

Resting time

30 minutes

Proofing time

45 minutes

Cooking time

30–40 minutes

Storage

Up to 2 days wrapped in a clean dish towel

Equipment

Stand mixer + dough hook

Instant-read thermometer

Bench scraper

Ingredients

Dough

Generous 1 tbsp (10 g) ground turmeric

3½ cups (15 oz./420 g) white bread flour (T65)

1 cup + 2 tsp (260 g/260 ml) water

1½ tsp (8 g) salt

0.25 oz. (5 g) fresh yeast

1.5 oz. (40 g) ripe liquid levain (see technique p. 40)

To finish

Olive oil, for brushing

3.5 oz. (100 g) poppy seeds

PREPARING THE DOUGH

Knead all the dough ingredients in the bowl of the stand mixer on low speed for 8 minutes until well combined. Increase the speed to medium and knead for 2 minutes. Make sure the dough temperature does not exceed 75°F (24°C). Place in a clean bowl, cover with plastic wrap, and let ferment for 1 hour at room temperature. Fold the dough once halfway through the fermentation time, after 30 minutes (see technique p. 48). Divide the dough into 4 pieces: 2 weighing 9.5 oz. (270 g) each and 2 weighing 3.5 oz. (100 g) each. Shape the pieces into balls and let rest for 30 minutes at room temperature.

SHAPING AND PROOFING THE DOUGH

Roll each 3.5-oz. (100-g) ball of dough into a 7-in. (18-cm) disk. Brush the disks with olive oil and cover them with poppy seeds. Using the bench scraper, cut a 4-in. (10-cm) cross in the center of each one. Shape the 9.5-oz. (270-g) pieces of dough into balls again, brush them with olive oil, and place seam side up in the center of the dough disks. Wrap the dough disks around the balls. Place with the crosses facing up on a baking sheet lined with parchment paper. Let proof in a steam oven set to 75°F (24°C), or on a rack in a turned-off oven above a bowl of boiling water, for 45 minutes.

BAKING THE TURMERIC BREAD

Place a rack in the center of the oven and another rack directly below it. Place a heavy-duty rimmed baking sheet on the bottom rack and preheat the oven to 475°F (240°C/Gas Mark 9). Bring 1 cup (250 ml) water to a simmer. Place the loaves on the baking sheet in the oven and carefully pour the simmering water into the rimmed sheet on the lower rack to create steam. Quickly close the oven door and bake the loaves for 30–40 minutes. Immediately transfer the loaves to a rack and let them cool completely at room temperature.

CHOCOLATE BREAD

Pain au cacao

Makes 6 loaves, weighing 7.75 oz. (220 g) each

Active time

1½ hours

Autolyse time

30 minutes

Bulk fermentation time

1 hour

Resting time

30 minutes

Proofing time

45 minutes–1 hour

Cooking time

15 minutes

Storage

Up to 24 hours wrapped in a clean dish towel

Equipment

Stand mixer + dough hook

Instant-read thermometer

Bread lame

Ingredients

Poolish

0.1 oz. (2 g) fresh yeast, crumbled

Scant ½ cup (100 g/100 ml) water

¾ cup + 2 tbsp (3.5 oz./100 g) white bread flour (T65)

Scant ½ tsp (2 g) salt

Dough

4 cups + 2 tbsp (1 lb. 2 oz./500 g) white bread flour (T65)

1⅓ cups (315 g/315 ml) water

Poolish (see above)

1¾ tsp (9 g) salt

0.1 oz. (2 g) fresh yeast

2 tsp (10 g/10 ml) water (for *bassinage*)

Chocolate flavoring

0.05 oz. (1 g) fresh yeast

Generous ⅓ cup (1.5 oz./40 g) unsweetened cocoa powder

2 tbsp (25 g) sugar

⅓ cup (90 g/90 ml) water (for *bassinage*)

7 oz. (200 g) dark couverture chocolate, 70% cacao

PREPARING THE CHOCOLATE BREAD DOUGH

Using the poolish and dough ingredients listed, prepare the traditional baguette dough with poolish (see recipe p. 128), up to the end of the kneading stage and before bulk fermentation. With the mixer running on low speed, add the 0.05 oz. (1 g) fresh yeast, cocoa powder, and sugar, then gradually add the ⅓ cup (90 g/90 ml) water. Increase the speed to high until the water is absorbed and the dough is smooth (*bassinage*). Cut the chocolate into approximately ½ -in. (1-cm) pieces and add to the bowl. Mix briefly on low speed. If it seems to be taking too long to incorporate the chocolate, finish mixing it in manually to avoid breaking it into tiny pieces. Make sure the dough temperature does not exceed 77°F (25°C). Place the dough in a clean bowl, cover with plastic wrap, and let ferment for 1 hour at room temperature, folding once after 30 minutes (see technique p. 48). Divide the dough into 6 pieces weighing 7.75 oz. (220 g) each, and gently shape each one into a ball. Cover with plastic wrap and let rest for 30 minutes at room temperature.

SHAPING AND PROOFING THE DOUGH

Flatten each piece of dough to burst any air bubbles and fold the top two-thirds down and the bottom two-thirds up. Fold in half to seal. Roll the dough against the work surface, pressing down gently on the ends to make slightly pointed tips. Place on a baking sheet lined with parchment paper. Let proof in a steam oven set to 75°F (24°C), or on a rack in a turned-off oven above a bowl of boiling water, for 45 minutes–1 hour.

SCORING AND BAKING THE CHOCOLATE BREAD

Place a rack in the center of the oven and another rack directly below it. Place a heavy-duty rimmed baking sheet on the bottom rack and preheat the oven to 475°F (240°C/Gas Mark 9). Bring 1 cup (250 ml) water to a simmer. Using the bread lame, score each loaf down the center lengthwise. Place in the oven and carefully pour the simmering water into the rimmed sheet on the lower rack to create steam. Quickly close the oven door and bake for about 15 minutes. Immediately transfer the loaves to a rack and let them cool completely at room temperature.

CHEFS' NOTES

Take care not to overbake this bread.
Since it is impossible to rely on the color, look for signs that the exterior is dry, but not hard. It is a light *viennoiserie*-type loaf and should not have a crisp crust.

TIGER BREAD

Pain à la bière

Makes 2 loaves, weighing about 1 lb. (450 g) each

Active time
1½ hours

Poolish fermentation time
Overnight

Bulk fermentation time
1½ hours

Resting time
20 minutes + 30 minutes

Proofing time
1–1¼ hours

Cooking time
30–40 minutes

Storage
Up to 2 days wrapped in a clean dish towel

Equipment
Stand mixer + dough hook
Instant-read thermometer
Offset spatula

Ingredients

Poolish
Scant 1 cup (225 g/225 ml) blonde beer
0.1 oz. (2 g) fresh yeast, crumbled
1¾ cups (8 oz./225 g) white bread flour (T65)

Beer bread dough
1¾ cups (8 oz./225 g) white bread flour (T65)
Scant ½ cup (1.75 oz./50 g) stoneground white whole wheat flour (T80)
15.75 oz. (447 g) poolish (see above)
0.1 oz. (3 g) fresh yeast
Scant ½ cup (100 g/100 ml) blonde beer
1¾ tsp (9 g) salt
3½ tbsp (50 g/50 ml) water (for *bassinage*)

Crackle topping
Scant ½ cup (1.75 oz./50 g) rye flour (T130)
Scant ⅓ cup (85 g/85 ml) water
0.1 oz. (2 g) fresh yeast
Scant ¼ tsp (1 g) salt

Decoration
White bread flour (T65)

PREPARING THE POOLISH (1 DAY AHEAD)
Using the ingredients listed, prepare the poolish, swapping out the water for beer (see technique p. 42). Let ferment overnight in the refrigerator.

PREPARING THE BEER BREAD DOUGH
The next day, knead all the dough ingredients, except the water, in the bowl of the stand mixer on low speed for 8 minutes until combined. Increase the speed to medium and continue to mix for 2 minutes. Gradually add the 3½ tbsp (50 g/50 ml) water as needed, depending on the consistency of the dough, which should be soft (*bassinage*). Make sure the dough temperature does not exceed 75°F (24°C). Place in a clean bowl, cover with plastic wrap, and let ferment for 1½ hours at room temperature. Fold the dough once halfway through the fermentation time, after 45 minutes (see technique p. 48). Divide the dough into 2 equal pieces and gently shape each one into a ball. Let rest for 20 minutes at room temperature.

SHAPING AND PROOFING THE DOUGH
Roll the dough into balls again, then roll each one out into an 8-in. (20-cm) square, with a thickness of ¼ in. (5 mm), leaving the corners rounded. Turn the squares 45° so the corners are at the top, bottom, and sides (diamond shape). Fold the right and left edges in toward the center to form the top corner of an isosceles triangle, then fold the remaining section at the bottom into the center to form the shorter side of the triangle. Place the loaves on a baking sheet lined with parchment paper, with the folds facing downward. Cover loosely with a towel or plastic wrap and let proof for 1–1¼ hours at room temperature.

PREPARING THE CRACKLE TOPPING
Stir together all the ingredients until well combined. Let rest for 30 minutes at room temperature before using.

BAKING THE LOAVES
Preheat the oven to 480°F (250°C/Gas Mark 8–9). Using the offset spatula, spread the crackle topping over the dough triangles in an even layer. Dust with bread flour, place in the oven on the baking sheet, and bake for 30–40 minutes. Immediately transfer the bread to a rack and let cool at room temperature.

CIABATTAS

Makes 5 ciabattas, weighing 7 oz. (200 g) each

Active time

1½ hours

Autolyse time

30 minutes–1 hour

Bulk fermentation time

2 hours

Proofing time

20 minutes

Cooking time

12–14 minutes

Storage

Up to 24 hours wrapped in a clean dish towel

Equipment

Stand mixer + dough hook

Instant-read thermometer

Bench scraper

Baker's couche (optional)

Heavy-duty baking sheet or baking stone

Ingredients

Ciabatta dough

4 cups + 2 tbsp (1 lb. 2 oz./500 g) white bread flour (T65)

1⅓ cups (320 g/320 ml) water

3.5 oz. (100 g) ripe liquid levain (see technique p. 40)

0.25 oz. (5 g) fresh yeast

1¾ tsp (9 g) salt

Bassinage

2 tbsp + 1 tsp (35 g/35 ml) water

2½ tbsp (35 g/38 ml) olive oil

To shape

Fine semolina flour

Olive oil

PREPARING THE DOUGH

Knead the flour and water in the bowl of the stand mixer on low speed for 5 minutes until no dry bits remain. Cover the bowl with plastic wrap or a dish towel and let rest for 30 minutes–1 hour at room temperature (autolyse). Add the levain, fresh yeast, and salt. Knead on low speed for 5 minutes until well combined. Increase the speed to high and knead for 3 minutes until the dough is supple, smooth, and elastic. Gradually add the water and oil for the *bassinage* stage, kneading on high speed after each addition until incorporated. Make sure the dough temperature does not exceed 77°F (25°C). Place the dough in a clean bowl lightly greased with olive oil and cover with plastic wrap. Let the dough ferment for 30 minutes at room temperature and perform a fold (see technique p. 48). Let ferment for another 30 minutes, then perform a second and final fold. Let the dough ferment undisturbed for an additional 1 hour at room temperature.

SHAPING AND PROOFING THE DOUGH

Dust the work surface with fine semolina flour. Scrape the dough out of the bowl onto the semolina flour and sprinkle more over the top. Divide the dough into 5 pieces weighing 7 oz. (200 g) each. Flatten them slightly, then wrinkle the tops using your fingertips, in order to form little creases. Place the dough smooth side up on a baking sheet lined with a floured baker's couche or clean dish towel. Let proof in a steam oven set to 75°F (24°C), or on a rack in a turned-off oven above a bowl of boiling water, for 20 minutes.

BAKING THE CIABATTAS

Place a heavy-duty baking sheet or baking stone on a rack in the center of the oven and a heavy-duty rimmed baking sheet on the bottom rack. Preheat the oven to 480°F (250°C/Gas Mark 9). Bring 1 cup (250 ml) water to a simmer. Invert the dough onto parchment paper, then slide the parchment paper onto the hot baking sheet in the center of the oven and carefully pour the simmering water into the rimmed sheet on the lower rack to create steam. Quickly close the oven door and bake for 12–14 minutes, or until the ciabattas are just beginning to color. Immediately transfer to a rack and let cool completely at room temperature.

CHEFS' NOTES

With a larger particle size than flour, fine semolina makes it easier to shape wet ciabatta dough. The dough has less contact with the work surface so sticks less. Semolina also adds crisp texture to the bread after baking.

BLACK BREAD

Pain noir

Makes 3 loaves, weighing 1 lb. 6 oz. (630 g) each

Active time

1½ hours

Soaking time

At least 1 hour (or overnight)

Bulk fermentation time

1 hour

Proofing time

20 minutes

Cooking time

50–55 minutes

Storage

Up to several days in the refrigerator well covered with plastic wrap

Equipment

Stand mixer + dough hook

Instant-read thermometer

Bowl scraper

3 loaf pans, 7 × 3 in. (18 × 8 cm), 3 in. (8 cm) deep

Ingredients

Seed, dried fruit, and nut mixture

½ cup (2.5 oz./75 g) hulled sunflower seeds

½ cup (2.5 oz./75 g) hulled pumpkin seeds (pepitas)

1½ cups (7 oz./200 g) whole hazelnuts

7 oz. (200 g) moist dried fruits of your choice (cranberries, prunes, apricots, etc.), roughly chopped if large

1 cup (250 g/250 ml) water

Bread dough

Scant 3 cups (10.5 oz./300 g) rye flour

1¾ cups (7 oz./200 g) whole wheat flour (T150)

1⅔ cups (400 g/400 ml) water at 158°F (70°C)

2¾ tsp (14 g) salt

0.25 oz. (7 g) fresh yeast

7 oz. (200 g) ripe liquid levain (see technique p. 40)

Soaked seed, dried fruit, and nut mixture (see above)

Flour for dusting

Oil for the pans

Decoration

1 cup (2.75 oz./80 g) rolled oats

CHEFS' NOTES

When this black bread is fresh, the crumb is very sticky and difficult to slice. It's best to wait until the next day before serving, as the bread loses its stickiness over time.

PREPARING THE SEED, DRIED FRUIT, AND NUT MIXTURE

Preheat the oven to 350°F (180°C/Gas Mark 4). Lightly toast the seeds and hazelnuts separately on a baking sheet lined with parchment paper (about 15 minutes each). Place the toasted seeds, nuts, and dried fruits in a bowl with the water. Let soak for at least 1 hour, or overnight, then drain.

PREPARING THE BREAD DOUGH

Knead the rye flour, whole wheat flour, water, and salt in the bowl of the stand mixer on low speed for 3 minutes to combine. Check the dough temperature: if it is below 122°F (50°C), add the fresh yeast and liquid levain, otherwise wait until it cools to this temperature. Continue kneading on low speed until well combined. Add the seed, nut, and dried fruit mixture, and knead until evenly mixed in. The dough will be soft and very sticky. Wet the bowl scraper and use to smooth the surface of the dough. Dust with a little flour to be able to assess how the fermentation is progressing: if the flour layer is still smooth, the dough has not fermented enough, but if the flour cracks, the dough is ready to be shaped. Cover with plastic wrap and let ferment for 1 hour until cracks form, making sure the dough temperature does not exceed 95°F (35°C).

SHAPING AND PROOFING THE LOAVES

Grease the loaf pans and coat the bottoms and sides with rolled oats. Wet the bowl scraper and use to divide the dough between the pans, placing about 1 lb. 6 oz. (630 g) in each one and filling them about two-thirds full. Cover with rolled oats and let proof for 20 minutes until cracks form on the surface.

BAKING THE LOAVES

Place a rack in the center of the oven and another rack directly below it. Place a heavy-duty rimmed baking sheet on the bottom rack and preheat the oven to 500°F (260°C/Gas Mark 10). Bring 1 cup (250 ml) water to a simmer. Place the loaves in the oven on the center rack and carefully pour the simmering water into the rimmed sheet on the lower rack to create steam. Quickly close the oven door and bake the loaves for 20 minutes, then reduce the heat to 425°F (220°C/Gas Mark 7) and continue to bake for an additional 20 minutes. Turn the loaves out of the pans and lower the oven temperature to 350°F (180°C/Gas Mark 4). Place the loaves back in the oven on the center rack for 10–15 minutes to dry the crust (open the oven door once or twice during this time to release any steam).

HAZELNUT BENOÎTONS

Benoîtons aux noisettes

Makes 16

Active time
1½ hours

Toasting time for flour and hazelnuts
35 minutes

Bulk fermentation time
30 minutes

Resting time
30 minutes in the refrigerator

Proofing time
1½ hours

Cooking time
8–10 minutes

Storage
Up to 2 days in a plastic bag

Equipment
Stand mixer + dough hook
Instant-read thermometer

Ingredients

1 cup + 2 tbsp (3½ oz./100 g) hazelnut flour

¾ cup (3½ oz./100 g) whole hazelnuts

3¼ cups (14 oz./400 g) white bread flour (T65)

Scant ½ cup (3.5 oz./100 g) lightly beaten egg (2 eggs), well chilled

⅔ cup (150 g/150 ml) whole milk, well chilled

0.5 oz. (15 g) fresh yeast, crumbled

1¾ tsp (9 g) salt

Scant ⅓ cup (2 oz./60 g) sugar

¼ cup (50 g/56 ml) hazelnut oil

3½ tbsp (50 g/50 ml) whole milk, well chilled (for *bassinage*)

Scant 1 cup (3½ oz./100 g) dried cranberries

PREPARING THE DOUGH

Preheat the oven to 350°F (180°C/Gas Mark 4). Spread the hazelnut flour over a baking sheet lined with parchment paper and toast for about 20 minutes until deeply golden; ensure it does not burn as any blackened bits will taste bitter. Spread the hazelnuts over a baking sheet lined with parchment paper and toast for about 15 minutes until dry, crisp, and golden in the center. Let cool and chop finely. Let cool completely before using. Knead the toasted hazelnut flour, bread flour, eggs, ⅔ cup (150 g/150 ml) milk, yeast, and salt in the bowl of the stand mixer for 5 minutes on low speed until well combined. Increase the speed to high and knead for 7–8 minutes until the dough is supple, smooth, and elastic. Add the sugar and hazelnut oil and mix until smooth. Incorporate the 3½ tbsp (50 g/50 ml) milk for *bassinage* as needed, depending on the consistency of the dough: it should be soft and sticky. With the mixer running on low speed, add the toasted hazelnuts and cranberries. Increase the speed to high and mix for 1 minute to ensure even distribution without crushing the hazelnuts and cranberries. If, at this point, they are not evenly distributed, finish mixing them in by hand, folding the dough several times. Make sure the dough temperature does not exceed 77°F– 79°F (25°C–26°C). Place in a clean bowl, cover with plastic wrap, and let ferment for 30 minutes at room temperature.

SHAPING AND PROOFING THE DOUGH

Flatten the dough into a rectangle measuring 9½ × 11¾ in. (24 × 30 cm), with a thickness of ¼ in. (5 mm). Place on a floured dish towel and let rest for 30 minutes in the refrigerator. Cut the dough into 16 rectangles measuring 1¼ × 6 in. (3 × 15 cm) and place on a baking sheet lined with parchment paper, with the floured side facing up. Let proof in a steam oven set to 75°F (24°C), or place on a rack in a turned-off oven above a bowl of boiling water, for 1½ hours.

BAKING THE BENOÎTONS

Place a rack in the center of the oven and another rack directly below it. Place a heavy-duty rimmed baking sheet on the bottom rack and preheat the oven to 475°F (240°C/Gas Mark 9). Bring 1 cup (250 ml) water to a simmer. Place the benoîtons on the baking sheet in the oven and carefully pour the simmering water into the rimmed sheet on the lower rack to create steam. Quickly close the oven door and bake the benoîtons for 8–10 minutes until they begin to color. They should remain soft and tender inside. Transfer to a rack and let cool.

BUCKWHEAT BREAD

Pain au sarrasin

Makes 2 loaves, weighing 1 lb. 2 oz. (500 g) each

Active time

1½ hours

Fermentation time

2½ hours

Bulk fermentation time

30 minutes + 10–12 hours in the refrigerator

Proofing time

1 hour

Cooking time

30–40 minutes

Storage

Up to 3 days

Equipment

Stand mixer + dough hook

Instant-read thermometer

Bread lame

Ingredients

Buckwheat levain

1.5 oz. (40 g) ripe stiff levain (see technique p. 38)

½ cup minus 1 tbsp (1.75 oz./50 g) buckwheat flour

3½ tbsp (50 g/50 ml) water at 95°F (35°C)

Dough

2¾ cups (12.5 oz./350 g) white bread flour (T65)

1⅓ cups (5.25 oz./150 g) stoneground white whole wheat flour (T80)

Scant 1½ cups (350 g/350 ml) water

2 tsp (10 g) salt

0.1 oz. (2 g) fresh yeast

5 oz. (140 g) buckwheat levain (see above)

PREPARING THE BUCKWHEAT LEVAIN (1 DAY AHEAD)

Mix all the ingredients in the bowl of the stand mixer fitted with the dough hook until well combined. Cover and let ferment in the bowl for 2½ hours at room temperature.

PREPARING THE DOUGH (1 DAY AHEAD)

Knead all the dough ingredients in the bowl of the stand mixer on low speed for 15 minutes until well combined. Make sure the dough temperature does not exceed 75°F (24°C). Place in a clean bowl, cover with plastic wrap, and let ferment for 30 minutes at room temperature. Perform a fold (see technique p. 48), cover with plastic wrap, and let rest for 10–12 hours in the refrigerator.

SHAPING AND PROOFING THE DOUGH

The next day, divide the dough into 2 pieces weighing 1 lb. 2 oz. (500 g) each. Shape each piece into an approximate 6 × 8-in. (15 × 20-cm) oblong. Place the loaves on a baking sheet lined with parchment paper, cover loosely with a towel or plastic wrap, and let proof for 1 hour at room temperature.

SCORING AND BAKING THE LOAVES

Place a rack in the center of the oven and another rack directly below it. Place a heavy-duty rimmed baking sheet on the bottom rack and preheat the oven to 480°F (250°C/Gas Mark 9). Bring 1 cup (250 ml) water to a simmer. Dust the loaves with flour and score with a crosshatch pattern (see technique p. 58). Place the loaves on the baking sheet in the oven and carefully pour the simmering water into the rimmed sheet on the lower rack to create steam. Quickly close the oven door and bake for 30–40 minutes. Immediately transfer to a rack and let cool at room temperature.

TWO-TONE SANDWICH BREAD

Pain de mie bicolore

Makes 3 loaves, weighing about 12 oz. (340 g) each

Active time
2 hours

***Pâte fermentée* fermentation time**
Overnight

Bulk fermentation time
45 minutes

Resting time
30 minutes

Proofing time
1¼–1½ hours

Cooking time
25–30 minutes

Storage
Up to 3 days wrapped in a clean dish towel

Equipment
Stand mixer + dough hook
Instant-read thermometer
3 Pullman (*pain de mie*) loaf pans, 3 × 7 in. (7 × 18 cm), 3¼ in. (8 cm) deep

Ingredients

Pâte fermentée
½ cup (2.5 oz./70 g) white bread flour (T65)
3 tbsp (43 g/43 ml) water
Scant ¼ tsp (1 g) salt
0.05 oz. (1 g) yeast

Sandwich bread dough
4 cups + 2 tbsp (1 lb. 2 oz./500 g) white bread flour (T65)
1 cup (250 g/250 ml) water
Scant ¼ cup (25 g) milk powder
2 tbsp (25 g) sugar
1 oz. (25 g) fresh yeast
2 tsp (10 g) salt
3 tbsp (1.75 oz./50 g) butter
4 oz. (115 g) *pâte fermentée* (see above)
1 oz. (25 g) bamboo charcoal powder
Butter for the pans

PREPARING THE PÂTE FERMENTÉE (1 DAY AHEAD)

Mix the flour, water, salt, and yeast together in the bowl of the stand mixer and knead on low speed, or by hand, for 10 minutes until smooth. Place in a bowl, cover with plastic wrap, and let ferment overnight in the refrigerator.

PREPARING THE SANDWICH BREAD DOUGH

Knead all the ingredients, except the bamboo charcoal powder, in the bowl of the stand mixer on low speed for 3 minutes until well combined. Increase the speed to high and knead for 7 minutes until the dough is supple and elastic. Remove the dough from the bowl and weigh out 1 lb. 2 oz. (500 g). Place this amount back in the bowl, add the bamboo charcoal powder, and knead on low speed for 2 minutes until completely incorporated. Make sure the dough temperature does not exceed 75°F (24°C). Shape the plain dough and the black dough into two separate balls, place in separate bowls, and cover with plastic wrap. Let ferment for 45 minutes at room temperature. Roll each ball of dough into a 12 × 20-in. (30 × 50-cm) rectangle. Let rest for 30 minutes in the refrigerator.

SHAPING AND PROOFING THE LOAVES

Grease the bases and lids of the loaf pans with butter. Brush the plain dough with a little water to moisten it and place the charcoal-colored dough on top. Roll them up together lengthwise, with the plain dough on the outside, and cut into 3 equal pieces. Place in the pans, seam side down, and cover with the lids. Let proof in a steam oven set to 75°F (24°C), or on a rack in a turned-off oven above a bowl of boiling water, for 1¼–1½ hours.

BAKING THE LOAVES

Preheat the oven to 425°F (220°C/Gas Mark 7) and bake the loaves for 25–30 minutes. Immediately turn the loaves out of the pans and let them cool completely on a rack.

JAPANESE MILK BREAD

Pain de mie au tangzhong

Makes 3 loaves, weighing 11.5 oz. (330 g) each

Active time

1½ hours

Fermentation time (for *tangzhong*)

At least 1 hour, or preferably overnight

Bulk fermentation time

30 minutes

Resting time

15 minutes

Cooking time

About 20 minutes

Storage

Up to several days in a well-sealed plastic bag

Equipment

Instant-read thermometer

Stand mixer + dough hook

3 Pullman (*pain de mie*) loaf pans, 3 × 7 in. (8 × 18 cm), 3 in. (8 cm) deep

Ingredients

Tangzhong

Scant ½ cup (1.75 oz./50 g) all-purpose flour (*gruau*)

1¼ cups (300 g/300 ml) whole milk

Milk bread dough

4 cups + 2 tbsp (1 lb. 2 oz./500 g) all-purpose flour (*gruau*)

Scant ¼ cup (55 g/55 ml) whole milk, well chilled

12.5 oz. (350 g) *tangzhong* (see above)

2 tbsp (25 g) sugar

1 oz. (25 g) fresh yeast

2 tbsp (25 g) butter, diced, at room temperature

2 tsp (10 g) salt

Butter for the pans

PREPARING THE TANGZHONG (1 DAY AHEAD IF FERMENTING OVERNIGHT)

Combine the flour and milk in a saucepan and warm to 140°F (60°C), whisking continually until the mixture thickens and forms a paste. Transfer to an airtight container, cover, and let ferment in the refrigerator for at least 1 hour, or preferably overnight. This mixture is quite gelatinous and may release a little water on the surface.

PREPARING THE MILK BREAD DOUGH

Knead all the dough ingredients in the bowl of the stand mixer on low speed for 5 minutes until well combined. Increase the speed to high and knead for an additional 6 minutes until the dough is supple and elastic. Make sure the dough temperature does not exceed 73°F–77°F (23°C–25°C). Cover the bowl with plastic wrap and let ferment for 30 minutes at room temperature. Divide the dough into 9 pieces weighing 3.75 oz. (110 g) each. Flatten slightly and fold the four corners of each piece in toward the center, turn them over, and gently shape into balls. Let rest for 15 minutes at room temperature.

SHAPING AND PROOFING THE DOUGH

Grease the loaf pans and lids with butter. Flatten the dough balls to burst any air bubbles and roll them into 2 × 6-in. (5 × 15-cm) rectangles, 1/16 in. (2 mm) thick. Starting with a short end, fold in 3, like a letter. Rotate the dough 90° clockwise and roll out again into rectangles of the same size. Roll the pieces up tightly like jelly rolls and place 3 in each pan with the seams facing down and the coils facing the sides of the pans. Put the lids on and let proof for 1 hour in a steam oven set to 75°F (24°C), or on a rack in a turned-off oven above a bowl of boiling water.

BAKING THE LOAVES

Preheat the oven to 425°F (220°C/Gas Mark 7). Place the covered pans in the oven and bake for about 20 minutes, until uniformly golden. Immediately turn the loaves out of the pans and let them cool completely on a rack.

CHEFS' NOTES

The *tangzhong* method helps to retain more moisture in the dough. When cooking *tangzhong*, the starch in the flour absorbs a significant amount of liquid, locking it in.

Although it has 10% higher hydration, dough made with *tangzhong* has a similar consistency to that of a classic sandwich loaf.

Tangzhong-based bread is moister than a standard sandwich loaf so is softer and stays fresh longer.

STONEGROUND BREAD

Tourte de meule

Makes 2 loaves, weighing about 1 lb. 3 oz. (550 g) each

Active time

1½ hours

Autolyse time

30 minutes

Bulk fermentation time

2 hours

Resting time

30 minutes

Proofing time

12 hours

Cooking time

50 minutes

Storage

Up to 3 days wrapped in a clean dish towel

Equipment

Stand mixer + dough hook

Instant-read thermometer

2 × 8-in. (20-cm) round bannetons

Bread lame

Ingredients

Scant 4½ cups (1 lb. 2 oz./500 g) stoneground white whole wheat flour (T80)

1½ cups (375 g/375 ml) water

2 tsp (10 g) salt

0.1 oz. (2 g) fresh yeast

7 oz. (200 g) ripe stiff levain (see technique p. 38)

3½ tbsp (50 g/50 ml) water (for *bassinage*)

PREPARING THE DOUGH (1 DAY AHEAD)

Knead all the ingredients, except the levain and the 3½ tbsp (50 g/50 ml) water for the *bassinage* stage, in the bowl of the stand mixer on low speed for 3 minutes until well combined. Cover the bowl with plastic wrap and let rest for 30 minutes at room temperature (autolyse). Knead for an additional 10 minutes on low speed, followed by 2 minutes on medium speed, until the dough is supple and smooth. Gradually add the 3½ tbsp (50 g/50 ml) water as needed, depending on the consistency of the dough, which should be supple (*bassinage*). Make sure the dough temperature does not exceed 77°F (25°C). Cover the bowl with plastic wrap and let ferment for 2 hours at room temperature, folding the dough once after 45 minutes (see technique p. 48) and a second time 45 minutes later. After the final 30 minutes, divide the dough into 2 pieces weighing 1 lb. 3 oz. (550 g) and gently shape each piece into a ball. Let rest for 30 minutes at room temperature.

SHAPING AND PROOFING THE DOUGH (1 DAY AHEAD)

Flour the bannetons. Shape each piece of dough into a loose boule (see technique p. 50) and place seam side up in the bannetons. Place the bannetons in loose-fitting plastic bags, seal shut, and let proof for 12 hours in the refrigerator.

BAKING THE LOAVES

The next day, place a rack in the center of the oven and another rack directly below it. Place a heavy-duty rimmed baking sheet on the bottom rack and preheat the oven to 480°F (250°C/Gas Mark 9). Bring 1 cup (250 ml) water to a simmer. Remove the bannetons from the plastic bags and quickly invert them onto a baking sheet lined with parchment paper. Using the bread lame, score the dough with a square shape and make fine decorative lines in the center, if you wish. Place the loaves on the baking sheet in the oven, carefully pour the simmering water into the rimmed sheet on the lower rack to create steam, and quickly close the oven door. Bake for 30 minutes at 480°F (250°C/Gas Mark 9), followed by 20 minutes at 425°F (220°C/Gas Mark 7). Immediately transfer the loaves to a rack and let them cool completely at room temperature.

PRETZELS

Bretzels

Makes 8

Active time

2 hours

Bulk fermentation time

15 minutes

Resting time

15 minutes

Proofing time

1–1¼ hours

Cooking time

15 minutes + poaching the pretzels

Storage

Up to 2 days wrapped in a clean dish towel

Equipment

Stand mixer + dough hook

Instant-read thermometer

Ingredients

Pretzel dough

4 cups + 2 tbsp (1 lb. 2 oz./500 g) white bread flour (T65)

1 cup (250 g/250 ml) whole milk

1¾ tsp (9 g) salt

5 tbsp (3 oz./80 g) butter, diced, at room temperature

0.75 oz. (20 g) fresh yeast

2½ tsp (10 g) superfine sugar

5.25 oz. (150 g) ripe liquid levain (see technique p. 40)

4½ tsp (20 g/22 ml) sunflower oil

Poaching liquid

4 cups (1 kg/1 liter) water

¼ cup (1.75 oz./55 g) baking soda

Egg wash

1 egg white

Topping

Fleur de sel

PREPARING THE DOUGH

Knead all the pretzel dough ingredients in the bowl of the stand mixer on low speed for 3 minutes until well combined. Increase the speed to medium and knead for 10 minutes until the dough is supple and elastic. Make sure the dough temperature does not exceed 75°F (24°C). Cover with plastic wrap and let ferment for 15 minutes at room temperature. Divide the dough into 8 pieces weighing 3.75 oz. (105 g) each and shape them into balls. Let rest for 15 minutes at room temperature.

SHAPING AND PROOFING THE DOUGH

Using your hands, roll each ball of dough into a rope measuring 10–12 in. (25–30 cm) in length. To shape each rope into a pretzel, hold both ends of the rope and cross them once to make a loop. Cross a second time and fold the ends up over the top edge of the loop. Press down to seal well. Place the pretzels on a baking sheet lined with parchment paper. Let proof in a steam oven set to 75°F (24°C), or on a rack in a turned-off oven above a bowl of boiling water, for 15–30 minutes, followed by 45 minutes in the refrigerator.

COOKING THE PRETZELS

Preheat the oven to 425°F (220°C/Gas Mark 7). Prepare the poaching liquid by combining the water and baking soda in a large saucepan. Bring to a boil and maintain at a simmer over low heat. Poach the pretzels in the simmering water for about 30 seconds on each side. Remove with a slotted spoon and return them to the parchment-lined baking sheet. Lightly whisk the egg white and brush over the pretzels. Sprinkle with fleur de sel and bake for about 15 minutes, until golden.

SPICED BREAD STARS

Étoiles de pain d'épice

Makes 16

Active time

1½ hours

Fermentation time for mother dough

At least overnight, or up to 3 weeks

Freezing time

30 minutes

Cooking time

About 10 minutes

Storage

Up to several days in an airtight container

Equipment

Instant-read thermometer

Stand mixer + paddle beater or spatula

3-in. (8-cm) star-shaped cookie cutter

Ingredients

Mother dough (*pâte mère*)

Scant 1 cup (10.5 oz./300 g) honey

6.25 oz. (180 g) ripe liquid levain (see technique p. 40)

2⅓ cups (9 oz./250 g) rye flour

Spiced bread dough

¾ cup + 2 tbsp (3.5 oz./100 g) white bread flour (T65)

1 tsp (6 g) baking soda

1½ tsp (4 g) ground ginger

1½ tsp (4 g) quatre-épices spice mix

1½ tsp (4 g) ground cinnamon

Mother dough (see above)

3 tbsp (2 oz./50 g) lightly beaten egg (about 1 egg)

7 tbsp (3.5 oz./100 g) butter, browned (*beurre noisette*)

Finely grated zest of 1 orange

Butter for greasing

Lemon syrup glaze

2⅓ cups (10 oz./300 g) confectioners' sugar

⅓ cup (80 g/80 ml) lemon juice

Dough glaze

A little milk

PREPARING THE MOTHER DOUGH (AT LEAST 1 DAY AHEAD)

Heat the honey to 113°F (45°C) in a saucepan and pour into the bowl of the stand mixer. Add the remaining ingredients. Mix to combine (or stir by hand using a spatula). Let ferment for as long as possible: at least overnight, or up to 3 weeks (see Chefs' Notes).

PREPARING THE SPICED BREAD DOUGH

Sift together the flour, baking soda, and spices. Knead the mother dough, egg, browned butter, and orange zest in the bowl of the stand mixer on low speed to loosen. Add the sifted dry ingredients and mix until well blended. The dough will be soft and very sticky. Grease one side of two sheets of parchment paper with butter. Place the dough between the buttered sides of the sheets and roll it into an approximate 12-in. (30-cm) square, with a thickness of ⅓ in. (8 mm). Freeze the dough for 30 minutes to firm it up (it will be too sticky to cut out the stars at this point).

PREPARING THE LEMON GLAZE

Stir together the confectioners' sugar and lemon juice until smooth. Set aside at room temperature.

SHAPING AND BAKING THE STARS

When the dough is sufficiently firm, preheat the oven to 300°F (150°C/Gas Mark 2). Cut out 16 stars using the cutter and place on a baking sheet lined with parchment paper. Brush with a little milk to glaze and bake for about 8 minutes.

GLAZING THE SPICED BREAD STARS

As soon as you remove the stars from the oven, reduce the oven temperature to 195°F (90°C/gas on lowest setting). Immediately brush the stars with the lemon glaze and place in the oven for 2–3 minutes to ensure the glaze is no longer sticky.

CHEFS' NOTES

The longer fermentation time not only enhances the flavor of the spices, but also makes the stars moister and improves their keeping quality.

EINKORN BREAD

Pain au petit épeautre

Makes 3 loaves, weighing about 13.5 oz. (385 g) each

Active time

1½ hours

***Pâte fermentée* fermentation time**

Overnight

Autolyse time

30 minutes

Bulk fermentation time

30 minutes + overnight in the refrigerator

Resting time

45 minutes

Proofing time

45 minutes–1 hour

Cooking time

30 minutes

Storage

Up to 2 days wrapped in a clean dish towel

Equipment

Stand mixer + dough hook

Instant-read thermometer

3 loaf pans, 3 × 7 in. (7 × 18 cm), 3 in. (8 cm) deep

Bread lame (optional)

Ingredients

Pâte fermentée

⅔ cup + 1 tbsp (3 oz./90 g) white bread flour (T65)

Scant ¼ cup (56 g/56 ml) water

¼ tsp (1.5 g) salt

0.05 oz. (1.5 g) fresh yeast

Bread dough

4 cups + 2 tbsp (1 lb. 2 oz./500 g) einkorn flour

Scant 1½ cups (360 g/360 ml) water at 160°F (70°C)

2 tsp (10 g) salt

0.1 oz. (3 g) fresh yeast

5.25 oz. (150 g) ripe stiff levain (see technique p. 38)

5.25 oz. (150 g) *pâte fermentée* (see above)

PREPARING THE PÂTE FERMENTÉE (2 DAYS AHEAD)

Mix the flour, water, salt, and yeast together in the bowl of the stand mixer and knead on low speed, or by hand, for 10 minutes until smooth. Place in a bowl, cover with plastic wrap, and let ferment overnight in the refrigerator.

PREPARING THE BREAD DOUGH (1 DAY AHEAD)

Knead the flour and water in the bowl of the stand mixer on low speed for 3 minutes until well combined. Cover the bowl with plastic wrap and let rest for 30 minutes at room temperature (autolyse). Add the salt, yeast, levain, and *pâte fermentée*, and knead on low speed for 8 minutes until combined. Increase the speed to high and knead for 2 minutes until the dough is supple. Make sure the dough temperature does not exceed 77°F (25°C). Cover the bowl with plastic wrap and let ferment for 30 minutes at room temperature. Perform a fold (see technique p. 48), cover with plastic wrap, and let ferment in the refrigerator overnight.

SHAPING AND PROOFING THE DOUGH

The next day, remove the dough from the refrigerator 45 minutes before shaping. Divide the dough into 3 equal pieces and shape each one into a *bâtard* (see technique p. 51), 7 in. (18 cm) in length. Transfer to the loaf pans and let proof for 45 minutes–1 hour in a steam oven set to 75°F (24°C), or on a rack in a turned-off oven above a bowl of boiling water.

BAKING THE LOAVES

Place a rack in the center of the oven and another rack directly below it. Place a heavy-duty rimmed baking sheet on the bottom rack and preheat the oven to 480°F (250°C/Gas Mark 9). Bring 1 cup (250 ml) water to a simmer. Using the bread lame, score the tops of the loaves diagonally, if you wish. Place the pans in the oven, carefully pour the simmering water into the rimmed sheet on the lower rack to create steam, and quickly close the oven door. Bake for 20 minutes, then lower the heat to 425°F (220°C/Gas Mark 7) and continue to bake for an additional 10 minutes. Immediately turn the loaves out of the pans onto a rack and let them cool completely at room temperature.

SPELT BREAD

Pain au grand épeautre

Makes 2 loaves, weighing about 1 lb. 3 oz. (550 g) each

Active time

1½ hours

***Pâte fermentée* fermentation time**

Overnight

Bulk fermentation time

1½ hours

Resting time

30 minutes in the refrigerator

Proofing time

12–16 hours

Cooking time

40–45 minutes

Storage

Up to 3 days wrapped in a clean dish towel

Equipment

Stand mixer + dough hook

Instant-read thermometer

2 × 8-in. (20-cm) round bannetons

Bread lame (optional)

Ingredients

Pâte fermentée

¾ cup (3 oz./90 g) white bread flour (T65)

Scant ¼ cup (56 g/56 ml) water

¼ tsp (1.5 g) salt

0.05 oz. (1.5 g) fresh yeast

Bread dough

5 cups (1 lb. 2 oz./500 g) spelt flour, plus extra for shaping

Scant 1½ cups (350 g/350 ml) water at 160°F (70°C)

2 tsp (11 g) salt

0.05 oz. (1 g) fresh yeast

5.25 oz. (150 g) ripe stiff levain (see technique p. 38)

5.25 oz. (150 g) *pâte fermentée* (see above)

3½ tbsp (50 g/50 ml) water (for *bassinage*)

PREPARING THE PÂTE FERMENTÉE (2 DAYS AHEAD)

Mix the flour, water, salt, and yeast together in the bowl of the stand mixer and knead on low speed, or by hand, for 10 minutes until smooth. Place in a bowl, cover with plastic wrap, and let ferment overnight in the refrigerator.

PREPARING THE BREAD DOUGH (1 DAY AHEAD)

Knead all the ingredients, except the 3½ tbsp (50 g/50 ml) water for the *bassinage* stage, in the bowl of the stand mixer on low speed for 6 minutes until well combined. Increase the speed to medium and knead for 3 minutes until the dough is supple and smooth. Gradually add the 3½ tbsp (50 g/50 ml) water as needed, depending on the consistency of the dough, which should be supple. Make sure the dough temperature does not exceed 77°F (25°C). Place in a clean bowl, cover with plastic wrap, and let ferment for 45 minutes at room temperature. Fold the dough (see technique p. 48), cover again with plastic wrap, and let ferment for an additional 45 minutes. Perform a second fold, then shape the dough into a ball and let rest for 30 minutes in the refrigerator.

SHAPING AND PROOFING THE DOUGH (1 DAY AHEAD)

Divide the dough into 2 equal pieces, dust the work surface with spelt flour, and shape each piece into a boule (see technique p. 50). Place seam side down in the bannetons. Place the bannetons in loose-fitting plastic bags, seal shut, and let proof for 12–16 hours in the refrigerator.

BAKING THE SPELT BREAD

The next day, place a rack in the center of the oven and another rack directly below it. Place a heavy-duty rimmed baking sheet on the bottom rack and preheat the oven to 480°F (250°C/Gas Mark 9). Bring 1 cup (250 ml) water to a simmer. Remove the bannetons from the plastic bags and quickly invert them onto a baking sheet lined with parchment paper. Using the bread lame, score the tops of the loaves in the form of a cross, if you wish. Lower the oven temperature to 450°F (230°C/Gas Mark 8), place the loaves on the baking sheet in the oven, and carefully pour the simmering water into the rimmed sheet on the lower rack to create steam. Quickly close the oven door and bake for 40–45 minutes. Immediately transfer the loaves to a rack and let them cool completely at room temperature.

BREADSTICKS

Gressins

Makes about 20

Active time

1½ hours

Bulk fermentation time

30 minutes

Proofing time

30 minutes

Cooking time

30–35 minutes

Storage

Up to several days in an airtight container

Equipment

Stand mixer + dough hook

Instant-read thermometer

Ingredients

4 cups + 2 tbsp (1 lb. 2 oz./500 g) white bread flour (T65)

⅔ cup (160 g/160 ml) cold water

3.5 oz. (100 g) ripe liquid levain (see technique p. 40)

⅓ cup (75 g/80 ml) olive oil, plus extra for greasing

2½ tsp (10 g) sugar

0.35 oz. (10 g) fresh yeast

1¾ tsp (9 g) salt

Suggested toppings

Sesame seeds, poppy seeds, herbes de Provence, etc.

PREPARING THE DOUGH

Knead all the ingredients in the bowl of the stand mixer on low speed for 4 minutes until well combined. Do not overwork the dough (see Chefs' Notes): if it strengthens too much, it will be difficult to shape and will shrink while baking. Make sure the dough temperature does not exceed 68°F (20°C). Place in a clean bowl, cover with plastic wrap, and let ferment for 30 minutes at room temperature.

SHAPING AND PROOFING THE DOUGH

Divide the dough into 20 pieces weighing 1.5 oz. (40 g) each. Roll each piece into a 16-in. (40-cm) log and place on a baking sheet greased with olive oil. Brush the breadsticks with a little water and sprinkle with toppings of your choice. Let proof in a steam oven set to 75°F (24°C), or place on a rack in a turned-off oven above a bowl of boiling water, for about 30 minutes.

BAKING THE BREADSTICKS

Preheat the oven to 300°F (150°C/Gas Mark 2) and bake the breadsticks for 30–35 minutes, until dry. If they are thick, the center may still be soft, but the outside should be crisp.

CHEFS' NOTES

Avoid overworking the dough, as this can make the breadsticks tough, rather than light and crisp.

CRUMPETS

Makes 5

Active time
10 minutes

Cooking time
8 minutes

Storage
Up to 3 days in the refrigerator, covered with plastic wrap

Equipment
5 × 4-in. (10-cm) tart rings, 1 in. (2.5 cm) deep
Large skillet

Ingredients
10½ oz. (300 g) unrefreshed liquid levain (see technique p. 40 and Chefs' Notes)
1¼ tsp (6 g) sugar
¾ tsp (4 g) salt
1 tsp (4 g) baking powder
1 tbsp butter
Neutral oil of your choice

To serve (optional)
Butter
Jam of your choice
Chocolate spread (see technique p. 120)

PREPARING THE BATTER

Pour the levain into a bowl and add the sugar and salt. Whisk until well combined. Whisk in the baking powder. Wait a few minutes: the batter should start to bubble slightly.

COOKING THE CRUMPETS

Meanwhile, lightly grease the insides of the tart rings with the butter. Lightly grease the skillet with a few drops of neutral oil and warm it over medium heat. Place the rings in the skillet and divide the batter equally between them. Reduce the heat to low. Cover the skillet and cook over low heat for about 5 minutes until the tops of the crumpets are set and small holes form. Carefully turn the crumpets over, remove the rings (they should detach easily), and continue cooking for about 3 minutes until the undersides are golden.

Serve the crumpets warm. You can put them in the toaster to brown them more and make them crisp. Spread with butter and jam, or chocolate spread, if you wish. Serve hot.

CHEFS' NOTES

The levain should be relatively mild, like yogurt. If it is too sour, you can add a little more baking powder and sugar.

FLAKY ROLLS

Petits pains feuilletés

Makes 16 rolls, weighing about 2 oz. (60 g) each

Active time

2 hours

Bulk fermentation time

1 hour + 10–12 hours in the refrigerator

Resting time

1 hour

Proofing time

1½ hours

Cooking time

20 minutes

Storage

Up to 24 hours wrapped in a clean dish towel

Equipment

Stand mixer + dough hook

Instant-read thermometer

16 × 2½-in. (6.5-cm) round cake pans, 1½ in. (3.5 cm) deep

Ingredients

Water dough

4 cups + 2 tbsp (1 lb. 2 oz./500 g) all-purpose flour (*gruau*)

1 cup + 5 tsp (270 g/270 ml) water

1¾ tsp (9 g) salt

0.25 oz. (5 g) fresh yeast

Laminating butter

1 stick + 2 tbsp (5 oz./150 g) butter, preferably 84% fat

Butter for the pans

To finish

3 tbsp (1.75 oz./50 g) butter, melted and browned (*beurre noisette*)

Fleur de sel

PREPARING THE WATER DOUGH (1 DAY AHEAD)

Knead all the water dough ingredients in the bowl of the stand mixer on low speed for 5 minutes until well combined. Increase the speed to medium and knead for 5 minutes until the dough is supple and elastic. Make sure the dough temperature does not exceed 75°F (24°C). Place in a clean bowl, cover with plastic wrap, and let ferment for 1 hour at room temperature. Fold the dough once (see technique p. 48), shape it into a ball, and place in a clean bowl. Cover with plastic wrap and let ferment for 10–12 hours in the refrigerator.

LAMINATING THE DOUGH

The next day, roll the dough into a 6 × 12-in. (15 × 30-cm) rectangle. Roll the laminating (84%) butter into a 6-in. (15-cm) square (see technique p. 62). Place the butter in the center of the dough and fold the ends of the dough over it to meet in the center, enclosing the butter completely. Roll the dough into an approximate 8 × 20-in. (20 × 50-cm) rectangle. Fold the shorter ends of the dough over so that they meet in the center, then fold the dough in half, like a book, to make a double turn. Let rest for 15–30 minutes in the refrigerator. Give the dough a quarter turn clockwise. Roll the dough into an approximate 8 × 20-in. (20 × 50-cm) rectangle, then fold it in 3, like a letter, to make a single turn. Let rest for 30 minutes in the refrigerator.

SHAPING AND PROOFING THE DOUGH

Lightly grease the cake pans with butter and place on a baking sheet. Roll the dough into a 12½ × 21¼ in. (32 × 40-cm) rectangle and trim the edges all around. Roll the dough up from one long side into a tight log, then cut the log into 16 × 1-in. (2.5-cm) slices. Place the slices flat in the pans. Let proof in a steam oven set to 75°F (24°C), or on a rack in a turned-off oven above a bowl of boiling water, for 1½ hours.

BAKING THE FLAKY ROLLS

Preheat the oven to 450°F (230°C/Gas Mark 8) and bake the rolls for 20 minutes until puffed and golden. As soon as the rolls are removed from the oven, brush them with browned butter and sprinkle with a little fleur de sel. Let cool in the pans for 10 minutes before turning them out onto a rack to cool.

FLAKY RYE-WHEAT LOAF

Pain de méteil feuilleté

Makes 3 loaves, weighing 13 oz. (360 g) each

Active time

2 hours

***Pâte fermentée* fermentation time**

Overnight

Bulk fermentation time

30 minutes

Resting time

30 minutes

Chilling time

30 minutes

Proofing time

1½ hours

Cooking time

30 minutes

Storage

Up to 2 days wrapped in a clean dish towel

Equipment

Stand mixer + dough hook

Instant-read thermometer

3 loaf pans, 3 × 7 in. (7 × 18 cm), 3 in. (8 cm) deep

Ingredients

Pâte fermentée

¾ cup (3 oz./90 g) white bread flour (T65)

Scant ¼ cup (56 g/56 ml) water

¼ tsp (1.5 g) salt

0.05 oz. (1.5 g) fresh yeast

Rye-wheat dough

2⅓ cups (9 oz./250 g) rye flour (T130)

2 cups (9 oz./250 g) all-purpose flour (T55)

1⅓ cups (310 g/310 ml) water

1¾ tsp (9 g) salt

0.5 oz. (15 g) fresh yeast

5.25 oz. (150 g) *pâte fermentée* (see above)

Laminating butter

1 stick + 2 tsp (4.5 oz./125 g) butter, preferably 84% fat

Butter for the pans

PREPARING THE PÂTE FERMENTÉE (1 DAY AHEAD)

Mix the flour, water, salt, and yeast together in the bowl of the stand mixer and knead on low speed, or by hand, for 10 minutes until smooth. Place in a bowl, cover with plastic wrap, and let ferment overnight in the refrigerator.

PREPARING THE RYE-WHEAT DOUGH

Knead all the dough ingredients in the bowl of the stand mixer on low speed for 6 minutes until well combined. Increase the speed to high and knead for 5 minutes until the dough is supple and elastic. Make sure the dough temperature does not exceed 75°F (24°C). Place in a clean bowl, cover with plastic wrap, and let ferment for 30 minutes at room temperature. Roll the dough into a 6 × 12-in. (15 × 30-cm) rectangle. Cover with plastic wrap and let rest for 30 minutes in the refrigerator.

LAMINATING THE DOUGH

Roll the laminating (84%) butter into a 6-in. (15-cm) square (see technique p. 62). Place the butter in the center of the dough and fold the ends of the dough over it to meet in the center, enclosing the butter completely. Give the dough one double turn (see technique p. 65), then rotate the folded dough 90° clockwise and give it one single turn (see technique p. 64). Cover with plastic wrap and chill for 30 minutes.

SHAPING AND PROOFING THE DOUGH

Grease the loaf pans with butter. Roll the dough into a 16 × 20-in. (40 × 50-cm) rectangle, then roll it up from one long side into a tight log and cut it into 3 equal pieces. Place the pieces in the pans, seam side down. Using scissors, cut a deep zigzag pattern into the top of each loaf, reaching down to the center. Let proof in a steam oven set to 75°F (24°C), or on a rack in a turned-off oven above a bowl of boiling water, for about 1½ hours.

BAKING THE LOAVES

Preheat the oven to 425°F (220°C/Gas Mark 7) and bake the loaves for 30–40 minutes. Immediately turn the loaves out of the pans and let them cool completely on a rack.

GARLIC AND CHEESE NAANS

Naans au fromage

Makes 12

Active time

1½ hours

Bulk fermentation time

1 hour

Resting time

30 minutes

Cooking time

4 minutes per naan

Storage

1–2 hours wrapped in a clean damp dish towel

Equipment

Stand mixer + dough hook

Instant-read thermometer

Skillet

Ingredients

Naan dough

4 cups + 2 tbsp (1 lb. 2 oz./500 g) white bread flour (T65)

1 cup + 5 tsp (270 g/270 ml) water

3.5 oz. (100 g) ripe liquid levain (see technique p. 40)

¼ cup (2 oz./60 g) plain yogurt or *fromage frais*

1¾ tsp (9 g) salt

0.05 oz. (1 g) fresh yeast

Garlic ghee

3 tbsp (1.75 oz./50 g) butter

1 clove garlic

Cheese and garlic filling

12 cloves garlic

1 lb. 5 oz. (600 g) mozzarella

To cook and garnish

Neutral oil

Garlic ghee (see above), melted

A few leaves and sprigs cilantro

PREPARING THE NAAN DOUGH

Knead all the ingredients in the bowl of the stand mixer on low speed for 5 minutes until well combined. Increase the speed to high and knead for 8 minutes until the dough is supple and elastic. The dough temperature should be 73°F–75°F (23°C–24°C). Place in a clean bowl, cover with plastic wrap, and let ferment for 1 hour at room temperature. Divide the dough into 12 pieces weighing about 2.75 oz. (80 g) each and gently shape each piece into a ball. Cover with plastic wrap and let rest for 30 minutes at room temperature.

PREPARING THE GARLIC GHEE

Meanwhile, melt the butter in a saucepan over very low heat and let it simmer gently until a foamy white layer forms on top. Skim off as much of the foam from the surface as you can. When the butter is translucent, i.e., clarified, pour it carefully into a bowl, leaving the milk solids at the bottom of the pan. Chop the garlic very finely and stir it into the clarified butter.

SHAPING AND FILLING THE NAANS

Roll each piece of dough into a 7-in. (18-cm) round disk with a thickness of about 1⁄16 in. (2 mm). Place 1.75 oz. (50 g) mozzarella and 1 finely chopped clove garlic in the center of each one. Fold the dough in half to enclose the filling, sealing the edges well. Roll each piece into an approximate 4 × 12-in. (10 × 30-cm) oval and place on a sheet of parchment paper.

COOKING THE NAANS

Lightly grease the skillet with oil-soaked paper towels and heat it over medium heat. When the skillet is hot, cook one naan at a time for about 2 minutes on each side until golden. Cover the skillet as you cook each naan to keep it moist and, using a piece of parchment paper, carefully flip it by hand. Remove each naan from the pan as it cooks and immediately brush it with melted garlic ghee. Serve immediately garnished with cilantro leaves and sprigs. Alternatively, the naans can be stacked and wrapped in a damp dish towel for up to 2 hours.

FOUGASSE

Makes 3 fougasses, weighing about 12 oz. (330 g) each

Active time

1½ hours

Bulk fermentation time

1½ hours + overnight

Proofing time

30 minutes

Cooking time

14–16 minutes

Storage

Up to 24 hours well covered in plastic wrap

Equipment

Stand mixer + dough hook

Instant-read thermometer

Bench scraper

Ingredients

Fougasse dough

4 cups + 2 tbsp (1 lb. 2 oz./500 g) white bread flour (T65)

1⅓ cups (325 g/325 ml) water

2 tsp (10 g) salt

0.25 oz. (5 g) fresh yeast

3.5 oz. (100 g) ripe liquid levain (see technique p. 40)

Bassinage

2 tbsp (30 g/30 ml) water

2½ tbsp (35 g/38 ml) olive oil

To finish

Olive oil

PREPARING THE DOUGH (1 DAY AHEAD)

Knead all the dough ingredients in the bowl of the stand mixer on low speed for 3 minutes until well combined. Increase the speed to medium and knead for 5 minutes until supple. Gradually add 2 tbsp (30 g/30 ml) water and 2½ tbsp (35 g/38 ml) olive oil as needed, depending on the consistency of the dough, which should be soft and supple (*bassinage*). Make sure the dough temperature does not exceed 75°F (24°C). Cover the bowl with plastic wrap and let ferment for 1½ hours at room temperature, folding the dough once halfway through the fermentation time, after 45 minutes (see technique p. 48). Shape the dough into a ball, place in a clean bowl, and cover with plastic wrap. Let ferment overnight in the refrigerator.

SHAPING AND PROOFING THE DOUGH

The next day, divide the dough into 3 pieces weighing about 12 oz. (330 g) each. Shape each one into a leaf-shaped triangle, 12 in. (30 cm) long, 8 in. (20 cm) wide, and about ½ in. (1 cm) thick. Place on a baking sheet lined with parchment paper. Using the bench scraper, make several slits in each piece of dough, cutting all the way through to make a leaf-like pattern. Using your fingers, stretch the slits open wide to prevent them from closing up during baking. Let proof in a steam oven set to 75°F (24°C), or on a rack in a turned-off oven above a bowl of boiling water, for 30 minutes.

BAKING THE FOUGASSES

Place a rack in the center of the oven and another rack directly below it. Place a heavy-duty rimmed baking sheet on the bottom rack and preheat the oven to 500°F (260°C/Gas Mark 10). Bring 1 cup (250 ml) water to a simmer. Place the fougasses on the baking sheet in the oven and carefully pour the simmering water into the rimmed sheet on the lower rack to create steam. Quickly close the oven door and bake for 14–16 minutes. As soon as the fougasses are removed from the oven, brush them with olive oil. Serve warm or transfer to a rack and let cool.

VIENNOISERIE

ALMOND CROISSANTS

Croissant aux amandes

Makes 6

Active time
30 minutes

Cooking time
15 minutes

Storage
Up to 24 hours

Equipment
Large serrated knife
Pastry bag with a plain tip

Ingredients

Vanilla syrup
- 2 cups (500 g/500 ml) water
- 2⅔ cups (1 lb. 2 oz./500 g) superfine sugar
- 1 vanilla bean, split lengthwise and seeds scraped

Almond croissants
- 6 × 1-day-old croissants (see technique p. 77)
- Vanilla syrup (see above)
- 8.5 oz. (240 g) almond cream (see technique p. 114)
- Generous 1 cup (3.5 oz./100 g) sliced almonds
- Confectioners' sugar

PREPARING THE VANILLA SYRUP

Combine the water, sugar, and vanilla seeds in a saucepan. Bring to a boil, stirring to dissolve the sugar. Remove from the heat and let cool.

PREPARING THE ALMOND CROISSANTS

Preheat the oven to 350°F (180°C/Gas Mark 4). Using the serrated knife, cut the croissants in half horizontally. Quickly dip the croissant halves in the cooled syrup and place on a rack for a few minutes to let the excess liquid drip off.

Spoon the almond cream into the pastry bag. Place the bottom halves of the croissants on a baking sheet lined with parchment paper and pipe a layer of almond cream over each one. Place the tops on the croissants and pipe a little almond cream over them. Sprinkle with the sliced almonds and bake for 15 minutes.

Dust with confectioners' sugar and serve warm or at room temperature.

TWO-TONE CHOCOLATE CROISSANTS

Croissant bicolore au chocolat

Makes 8

Active time
2 hours

Bulk fermentation time
30 minutes

Resting time
45 minutes–1 hour

Proofing time
2½ hours

Cooking time
22–25 minutes

Storage
Up to 24 hours

Equipment
Stand mixer + dough hook
Instant-read thermometer

Ingredients

Two-tone croissant dough

Plain water dough
- 2 cups (9 oz./250 g) cake flour (T45)
- ½ cup (125 g/125 ml) whole milk
- 1 tsp (5 g) salt
- 0.35 oz. (10 g) fresh yeast
- 2 tsp (10 g) honey
- 2 tbsp (25 g) sugar
- Scant 2 tbsp (25 g) butter, diced, at room temperature

Chocolate water dough
- 2.75 oz. (80 g) plain water dough (see above)
- 1½ tbsp (10 g) unsweetened cocoa powder
- 2 tsp (10 g/10 ml) water
- 2 tsp (10 g) butter, at room temperature

Laminating butter
- 1 stick + 2 tbsp (5 oz./150 g) butter, preferably 84% fat

Egg wash
- 1 egg
- 1 egg yolk
- 2 tsp (10 g/10 ml) whole milk

PREPARING THE CROISSANT DOUGH

Knead all the plain water dough ingredients in the bowl of the stand mixer on low speed for 5 minutes until well combined. Increase the speed to high and knead for 8 minutes until the dough is supple and elastic. The dough temperature should be between 70°F (21°C) and 73°F (23°C). Remove from the bowl.

To prepare the chocolate water dough, weigh out 2.75 oz. (80 g) of the plain water dough and return it to the bowl of the stand mixer. Add the cocoa powder, water, and butter and knead on low speed until well combined. Roll the chocolate water dough into a 6-in. (15-cm) square. Cover with plastic wrap and chill until using.

Roll the plain water dough into a 6 × 12-in. (15 × 30-cm) rectangle, cover with plastic wrap and let ferment for 30 minutes in the refrigerator. Roll the laminating (84%) butter into a 6-in. (15-cm) square (see technique p. 62). Place the butter in the center of the dough and fold the ends of the dough over it to meet in the center and enclose the butter completely. Roll the dough into an approximate 6 × 20-in. (15 × 50-cm) rectangle (about ⅛ in./3–4 mm thick). Fold the shorter ends of the dough over so that they meet in the center, then fold the dough in half, like a book, to make a double turn. Let rest for 15–30 minutes in the refrigerator. Give the dough a quarter turn clockwise. Roll the dough into an approximate 6 × 20-in. (15 × 50-cm) rectangle, then fold it in 3, like a letter, to make a single turn. Place the chocolate water dough on top and cover with plastic wrap. Let rest for 30 minutes in the refrigerator.

SHAPING AND PROOFING THE CROISSANTS

Roll the doughs, with one still on top of the other, into a 10 × 14-in. (25 × 35-cm) rectangle. Trim the edges all around, then cut the rectangle crosswise into 4 smaller rectangles with the longer sides measuring approximately 3½ in. (8.5 cm). Cut each rectangle diagonally lengthwise to obtain triangles, then roll up each triangle from the base to the tip with the chocolate part facing outward. Place on a baking sheet lined with parchment paper. Let proof in a steam oven set to 75°F (24°C), or place on a rack in a turned-off oven above a bowl of boiling water, for about 2½ hours.

BAKING THE CROISSANTS

Preheat the oven to 400°F (200°C/Gas Mark 6). Whisk the egg wash ingredients together and brush over the croissants. Bake for 22–25 minutes.

PISTACHIO-CHOCOLATE SWIRLS

Roulé pistache et chocolat

Makes 8

Active time
2 hours

Bulk fermentation time
30 minutes

Resting time
45 minutes–1 hour

Proofing time
2 hours

Cooking time
22–25 minutes

Storage
Up to 24 hours

Equipment
Stand mixer + dough hook
Instant-read thermometer

Ingredients

Pistachio cream
- Scant ½ cup (100 g/100 ml) whole milk
- Scant 2 tbsp (25 g) pistachio paste
- 1 egg yolk
- 3¾ tsp (15 g) sugar
- 1 tbsp (10 g) cornstarch
- 2 tsp (10 g) butter, at room temperature

Yeasted puff pastry

Base dough (*détrempe*)
- 2 cups (9 oz./250 g) cake flour (T45)
- ½ cup (125 g/125 ml) whole milk
- 1 tsp (5 g) salt
- 0.35 oz. (10 g) fresh yeast
- 2 tsp (10 g) honey
- 2 tbsp (25 g) sugar
- Scant 2 tbsp (25 g) butter, diced, at room temperature

Laminating butter
- 1 stick + 2 tbsp (5 oz./150 g) butter, preferably 84% fat

To assemble
- 1 cup (5.75 oz./160 g) chocolate chips

Egg wash
- 1 egg
- 1 egg yolk
- 2 tsp (10 g/10 ml) whole milk

Decoration
- Scant ¾ cup (3.5 oz./100 g) pistachios, chopped

PREPARING THE PISTACHIO CREAM

Heat the milk and pistachio paste in a saucepan. Meanwhile, whisk together the egg yolk and sugar in a bowl until pale and thick, then whisk in the cornstarch. Whisking constantly, slowly pour one-third of the hot milk mixture into the egg yolk mixture. Pour the mixture back into the saucepan and bring to a gentle simmer, stirring constantly with a spatula. As soon as the first bubbles appear, remove from the heat. Add the butter and stir until completely smooth. Press plastic wrap over the surface and chill until using.

PREPARING THE YEASTED PUFF PASTRY

Knead all the base dough ingredients in the bowl of the stand mixer on low speed for 5 minutes until well combined. Increase the speed to high and knead for 8 minutes until the dough is supple and elastic. The dough temperature should be between 70°F (21°C) and 73°F (23°C). Roll the dough into a 6 × 12-in. (15 × 30-cm) rectangle, cover with plastic wrap and let ferment for 30 minutes in the refrigerator. Roll the laminating (84%) butter into a 6-in. (15-cm) square (see technique p. 62). Place the butter in the center of the dough and fold the ends of the dough over it to meet in the center, enclosing the butter completely. Roll the dough into an approximate 8 × 20-in. (20 × 50-cm) rectangle. Fold the shorter ends of the dough over so that they meet in the center, then fold the dough in half, like a book, to make a double turn. Let rest for 15–30 minutes in the refrigerator. Give the dough a quarter turn clockwise. Roll the dough into an approximate 8 × 20-in. (20 × 50-cm) rectangle, then fold it in 3, like a letter, to make a single turn. Let rest for 30 minutes in the refrigerator.

SHAPING AND PROOFING THE SWIRLS

Roll the dough into an 8 × 14-in. (20 × 35-cm) rectangle and trim the edges all around. Loosen the pistachio cream with a flexible spatula, then spread it into an even layer across the dough. Scatter the chocolate chips evenly over the top. Roll the dough up from one long side into a tight log, then cut the log into 8 slices, 1 in. (2.5 cm) thick. Set the slices flat on a baking sheet lined with parchment paper. Let proof for about 2 hours in a steam oven set to 82°F (28°C), or on a rack in a turned-off oven above a bowl of boiling water.

BAKING THE SWIRLS

Preheat the oven to 400°F (200°C/Gas Mark 6). Whisk the egg wash ingredients together and brush over the swirls. Sprinkle the chopped pistachios around the edges and bake for 22–25 minutes.

TWISTED CINNAMON ROLLS

Makes 8

Active time
2 hours

Bulk fermentation time
30 minutes

Freezing time
30 minutes

Chilling time
30 minutes

Proofing time
1½–2 hours

Cooking time
20 minutes

Storage
Up to 2 days in a plastic bag

Equipment
Stand mixer + dough hook
Instant-read thermometer
8 × 4-in. (10-cm) round molds, 1½ in. (4 cm) deep

Ingredients

Brioche dough

- 1 cup + 2 tbsp (5.25 oz./150 g) all-purpose flour (*gruau*)
- 2¾ cups (12.5 oz./350 g) white bread flour (T65)
- ⅔ cup (5.25 oz./150 g) lightly beaten egg (3 eggs), well chilled
- ⅔ cup (150 g/150 ml) whole milk
- Scant ⅓ cup (2 oz./60 g) sugar
- ⅔ oz. (20 g) fresh yeast
- 1¾ tsp (9 g) salt
- 1 stick + 2 tbsp (5 oz./150 g) butter, diced, at room temperature

Cinnamon cream

- 1 stick + 2 tbsp (5 oz./150 g) butter, left for 1 hour at room temperature or microwaved on medium power for 30 seconds
- 3 tbsp (1.5 oz./40 g) packed brown sugar
- 2 tbsp (18 g) ground cinnamon
- Generous ¼ cup (1.5 oz./45 g) cornstarch
- Butter for the molds

Glaze

- Generous 2¾ cups (13.25 oz./375 g) confectioners' sugar
- 6 tbsp (90 g/90 ml) water
- 1½ tsp (4 g) ground cinnamon

PREPARING THE BRIOCHE DOUGH

Knead all the dough ingredients, except the butter, in the bowl of the stand mixer on low speed for 5 minutes until well combined. Increase the speed to medium and knead for 6–8 minutes until the dough is supple and elastic. With the mixer running on medium speed, add the butter and knead until completely incorporated (6–8 minutes). Make sure the dough temperature does not exceed 77°F–79°F (25°C–26°C). Place the dough in a clean bowl, cover with plastic wrap, and let ferment for 30 minutes at room temperature. Fold the dough once (see technique p. 48), cover with plastic wrap, and freeze for 30 minutes. Roll the dough into a 9½ × 16-in. (24 × 40-cm) rectangle, just over ⅛ in. (4 mm) thick. Chill for 30 minutes before shaping.

PREPARING THE CINNAMON CREAM

Place the softened butter in a bowl and add the brown sugar, cinnamon, and cornstarch. Stir with a flexible spatula until well combined and smooth. Set aside at room temperature until using.

SHAPING AND PROOFING THE CINNAMON ROLLS

Grease the molds with butter and place on a baking sheet. Using a spatula, quickly spread the cinnamon cream over the dough rectangle before the cream firms up due to contact with the chilled dough. Fold the rectangle in half, forming an 8 × 9½-in. (20 × 24-cm) rectangle. Cut the rectangle into 8 strips measuring 1¼ × 8 in. (3 × 20 cm) each. Gently pull on both ends of each strip to stretch it out by about 4 in. (10 cm). To form a roll, twist the strip, then wrap it around two fingers and tuck the end into the center on top. Place in the prepared molds and let proof for 1½–2 hours at room temperature. The dough needs to relax before baking.

BAKING THE CINNAMON ROLLS

Preheat the oven to 300°F (150°C/Gas Mark 2) and bake the cinnamon rolls for about 15 minutes. Let them cool completely in the molds on a rack.

PREPARING THE GLAZE AND GLAZING THE CINNAMON ROLLS

Warm all the glaze ingredients together in a saucepan, stirring to dissolve the sugar. Let cool slightly before using. Preheat the oven to 195°F (90°C/gas on lowest setting). Turn the cinnamon rolls out of the molds and dip the tops into the glaze. Shake off any excess, place the rolls with their tops facing upward on a baking sheet, and return to the oven for 5 minutes to dry out the glaze.

FLAKY BRIOCHE

Brioche feuilletée

Makes 2 brioches, weighing about 12.5 oz. (350 g) each

Active time
2 hours

Bulk fermentation time
1 hour + 10–12 hours in the refrigerator

Resting time
45 minutes–1 hour

Proofing time
2 hours

Cooking time
25–30 minutes

Storage
Up to 2 days

Equipment
Stand mixer + dough hook
Instant-read thermometer
2 loaf pans, 2¾ × 7 in. (7 × 18 cm), 3 in. (8 cm) deep

Ingredients

Brioche dough
2 cups (9 oz./250 g) all-purpose flour (*gruau*)
⅔ cup (5.25 oz./150 g) lightly beaten egg (3 eggs)
1 tsp (5 g) salt
0.35 oz. (10 g) fresh yeast
6 tbsp (3 oz./90 g) butter, diced, at room temperature
2½ tbsp (1 oz./30 g) sugar

Laminating butter
1 stick + 2 tbsp (5 oz./150 g) butter, preferably 84% fat

Butter for the pans

Syrup
1 cup (250 g/250 ml) water
⅔ cup (4.5 oz./125 g) sugar

PREPARING THE BRIOCHE DOUGH (1 DAY AHEAD)
Knead all the dough ingredients, except the butter and sugar, in the bowl of the stand mixer on low speed for 5 minutes until well combined. Increase the speed to medium and knead for 6–8 minutes until the dough is supple and elastic. With the mixer running on medium speed, add the butter and sugar and knead until completely incorporated (6–8 minutes). Make sure the dough temperature does not exceed 75°F (24°C). Place in a clean bowl, cover with plastic wrap, and let ferment for 1 hour at room temperature. Fold the dough once (see technique p. 48), return it to the bowl, and cover with plastic wrap. Let ferment for 10–12 hours in the refrigerator.

LAMINATING THE BRIOCHE DOUGH
The next day, roll the dough into a 6 × 12-in. (15 × 30-cm) rectangle. Roll the 84% butter into a 6-in. (15-cm) square (see technique p. 62). Place the butter in the center of the dough and fold the ends of the dough over it to meet in the center, enclosing the butter completely. Roll the dough into an approximate 8 × 20-in. (20 × 50-cm) rectangle. Fold the shorter ends of the dough over so that they meet in the center, then fold the dough in half, like a book, to make a double turn. Let the dough rest in the refrigerator for 15–30 minutes. Place it on the work surface and give it a quarter turn to the right so the flap is on one side. Roll the dough again into an approximate 8 × 20-in. (20 × 50-cm) rectangle, then fold it in 3, like a letter, to make a single turn. Let rest again for 30 minutes in the refrigerator.

SHAPING AND PROOFING THE FLAKY BRIOCHES
Grease the loaf pans with butter. Roll the dough into a rectangle slightly larger than 8 × 21¼ in. (20 × 54 cm). Trim the edges to that size all around, then cut in half lengthwise to obtain 2 strips measuring 4 × 21¼ in. (10 × 54 cm). Brush a little water over each strip to moisten, then fold in half lengthwise to obtain 2 × 21¼-in. (5 × 54-cm) strips. Pleat each strip like an accordion and place in the prepared loaf pans. Let proof in a steam oven set to 75°F (24°C), or place on a rack in a turned-off oven above a bowl of boiling water, for 2 hours.

PREPARING THE SYRUP
Combine the water and sugar in a saucepan and bring to a boil, stirring until the sugar dissolves. Let cool before using.

BAKING THE FLAKY BRIOCHES
Preheat the oven to 350°F (180°C/Gas Mark 4) and bake the brioches for 25–30 minutes. As soon as they come out of the oven, turn the brioches out of the pans and brush them with the syrup to make them glossy.

CRUFFINS

Makes 8

Active time
3 hours

Bulk fermentation time
15 minutes

Freezing time
1¼ hours

Proofing time
2 hours

Cooking time
20 minutes

Storage
Up to 24 hours, but best served within a few hours

Equipment
Stand mixer + dough hook
Instant-read thermometer
8 × 3-in. (8-cm) muffin pans, 1½ in. (4 cm) deep
Pastry bag with a plain round tip

Ingredients

Yeasted puff pastry dough

Base dough (*détrempe*)
1 cup (4.25 oz./125 g) all-purpose flour (*gruau*)
1 cup (4.25 oz./125 g) white bread flour (T65)
⅔ cup (150 g/150 ml) whole milk
1 tsp (5 g) salt
0.5 oz. (12 g) fresh yeast
2½ tbsp (1 oz./30 g) sugar
2 tsp (10 g) butter
1 knife tip water-soluble powdered red food coloring

Laminating butter
1 stick + 2 tbsp (5 oz./150 g) butter, preferably 84% fat

Butter for the pans

Syrup
Scant ½ cup (100 g/100 ml) water
Scant ⅔ cup (4.25 oz./120 g) sugar

To finish
Superfine sugar, for dusting
Jam of your choice, for filling

PREPARING THE YEASTED PUFF PASTRY DOUGH

Knead all the base dough ingredients together in the bowl of the stand mixer on low speed for 5 minutes until well combined. Increase the speed to high and knead for 8 minutes until the dough is supple and elastic. The dough temperature should be between 70°F (21°C) and 73°F (23°C). Roughly roll out the dough, fold the edges in toward the center, and turn it over. Cover with plastic wrap and let ferment for 15 minutes in the refrigerator. Roll the laminating (84%) butter into a 6-in. (15-cm) square (see technique p. 62) and chill until using. Roll the dough into a 6 × 12-in. (15 × 30-cm) rectangle, cover with plastic wrap, and freeze for 30 minutes. Place the butter in the center of the dough and fold the ends of the dough over it to meet in the center, enclosing the butter completely. Roll the dough into a 6 × 12-in. (15 × 30-cm) rectangle and give it a single turn (see technique p. 64). Cover with plastic wrap and freeze for 15 minutes. Give the dough a quarter turn clockwise, roll it into a 6 × 12-in. (15 × 30-cm) rectangle again, and give it another single turn. Cover with plastic wrap and freeze for 30 minutes.

SHAPING AND PROOFING THE DOUGH

Roll the dough into a 10 × 12½-in. (25 × 32-cm) rectangle, ⅛ in. (4.5 mm) thick. Trim the edges and cut out 8 rectangles measuring 3 × 5 in. (7.5 × 12 cm) each. Cut each rectangle into 3 strips, 1 × 5 in. (2.5 × 12 cm) each. Place the 24 strips on a baking sheet lined with parchment paper, cover with plastic wrap, and freeze for 15 minutes to firm up the butter. Grease the muffin pans with butter. To shape the cruffins, place one strip on the work surface with a short side facing you. Place another strip on top, about ½ in. (1 cm) lower than the first one to form a step. Repeat with a third strip. Press the strips together with your fingertips and roll them up together from top to bottom. Lay flat and gently fold the loose end of each strip downward, making sure to keep the same space between them. Place in the muffin pans. Coat your index finger with flour and use to make a large hole in the center of each cruffin. Let proof for 2 hours at room temperature in a draft-free place.

PREPARING THE SYRUP

Combine the water and sugar in a saucepan and bring to a boil, stirring to dissolve the sugar. Remove from the heat.

BAKING AND FILLING THE CRUFFINS

Preheat the oven on fan setting to 325°F (160°C/Gas Mark 3). Bake the cruffins for 20 minutes. As soon as they come out of the oven, brush them with the syrup. Let them cool in the pans for 10 minutes before turning out onto a rack to cool. Once the cruffins have cooled completely, roll them in superfine sugar. Using the tip of a knife, open up the hole in the center of each cruffin. Spoon your jam of choice into the pastry bag and pipe into the cruffins to fill them completely.

KINGS' CAKE

Galette des rois

Serves 8

Active time
3 hours

Chilling time
24 hours

Freezing time
Overnight

Cooking time
40 minutes

Storage
Up to 2 days

Equipment
Pastry bag fitted with a plain ½-in. (10-mm) tip
Ceramic charm or dried bean
Pastry pincher

Ingredients

Puff pastry
¾ tsp (4 g) salt
Scant ½ cup (100 g/100 ml) cold water
Heaping 1 tbsp (10 g) confectioners' sugar, sifted
1⅔ cups (7 oz./200 g) all-purpose flour (T55), sifted
Scant 3 tbsp (1.5 oz./40 g) butter, melted and cooled
1 stick plus 2 tbsp (5 oz./140 g) butter, preferably 84% butterfat

Frangipane cream
3½ tbsp (1.75 oz./50 g) butter, at room temperature
¼ cup (1.75 oz./50 g) sugar
Scant 3 tbsp (1.5 oz./40 g) lightly beaten egg (about 1 egg), at room temperature
2 tsp (10 ml) whipping cream, 35% fat
½ cup (1.75 oz./50 g) almond flour
1 tsp (5 ml) rum
Few drops of vanilla extract
1 oz. (25 g) pastry cream (see technique p. 112)

Egg wash
Scant ¼ cup (1.75 oz./50 g) lightly beaten egg (about 1 egg)

Simple syrup
3 tbsp plus 1 tsp (50 g/50 ml) water
¼ cup (1.75 oz./50 g) sugar
2 tsp (10 ml) rum

MAKING THE PUFF PASTRY (1 DAY AHEAD)
Use the ingredients to make a 5-turn puff pastry (see technique p. 66), adding the sugar with the flour. Divide the dough into 2 × 9-oz. (250-g) squares. Fold the corners of the squares to the center, turn over and shape each into a ball. Flatten, cover in plastic wrap, and chill for 24 hours.

MAKING THE FRANGIPANE CREAM (1 DAY AHEAD)
Cream the butter and sugar together in a large mixing bowl until light. Mix in the egg and whipping cream and then stir in the almond flour, rum, and vanilla. Add the pastry cream and mix until well blended. Line a baking sheet with parchment paper and spoon the frangipane cream into the pastry bag. Pipe the cream in a tight spiral, 8 in. (20 cm) in diameter, on the baking sheet, starting at the center and working outwards. Tuck the charm or bean into the cream, cover with plastic wrap, and freeze overnight.

ASSEMBLING THE CAKE
The next day, roll out each disk of pastry, with the folds underneath, into 9-in. (23-cm) rounds. Turn one over so the folds are facing up (the cream will cover the folds) and brush the edges with water. Place the disk of frangipane cream in the center. Cover with the second puff pastry round, with the folds facing down and in contact with the cream. Press the pastry edges together using the pastry pincher to seal them and prevent the filling leaking out during baking. Dampen a baking sheet by brushing with water. Turn the cake over and lift it onto the sheet. Brush the pastry with egg wash and chill for 30 minutes. Preheat the oven to 375°F (190°C/Gas Mark 5). Brush with egg wash again and, using a paring knife, mark curved lines in the pastry, ¼ in. (6 mm) apart, starting at the center and working to the outside. Place in the oven, lower the temperature to 340°F (170°C/Gas Mark 3), and bake for 40 minutes.

PREPARING THE SIMPLE SYRUP
While the cake is baking, prepare the syrup. Heat the water and sugar in a saucepan over medium heat and, when the sugar has dissolved, bring to a boil. Remove from the heat and stir in the rum. As soon as the cake is taken out of the oven, brush it with a little syrup to give the pastry a nice sheen, without making it soggy. Serve warm or at room temperature.

SWEET BRETON PUFF PASTRIES

Kouign-amann

Makes 15

Active time
3 hours

Resting time
15–20 minutes

Bulk fermentation time
Overnight

Chilling time
2 hours

Proofing time
2½ hours

Cooking time
16–20 minutes

Storage
Up to 2 days
in an airtight container

Equipment
Stand mixer + dough hook
15 × 4-in. (10-cm) round silicone molds

Ingredients

Water dough

- 4 cups + 2 tbsp (1 lb. 2 oz./500 g) white bread flour (T65)
- 0.5 oz. (15 g) fresh yeast, crumbled
- 3¾ tsp (15 g) sugar
- 4 tsp (20 g) salt
- 3 tbsp (1.75 oz./50 g) butter, diced, at room temperature
- 1¼ cups (300 g/300 ml) whole milk

Laminating butter

- 3½ sticks (14 oz./400 g) butter, preferably 84% fat
- 1 cup (7 oz./200 g) sugar

Butter for the pans
Sugar for the pans

PREPARING THE WATER DOUGH (1 DAY AHEAD)

Knead all the ingredients in the bowl of the stand mixer on low speed for 3 minutes. Increase the speed to medium and knead for 7 minutes. Remove the dough from the bowl, shape it into a ball, and cover with plastic wrap. Let rest for 15–20 minutes at room temperature. Roll the dough into an 8 × 16-in. (20 × 40-cm) rectangle, cover with plastic wrap, and let ferment overnight in the refrigerator.

LAMINATING THE DOUGH

The next day, prepare the 84% butter for laminating (see technique p. 62). Roll it into a 12-in. (30-cm) square and chill for 30 minutes. Sprinkle the 1 cup (7 oz./200 g) sugar over the butter, then fold the four corners in toward the center. Roll the butter out again into an 8-in. (20-cm) square. Place the butter in the center of the water dough so that there are 4 in. (10 cm) of dough on either side. Fold the dough over the butter to meet in the center, obtaining a square. Roll the dough into an 8 × 24-in. (20 × 60-cm) rectangle with a short side facing you. Fold the shorter sides of the dough toward the center, one-third of the way down from the top and two-thirds up from the bottom, like a letter, to make a single turn. Rotate the dough 90° clockwise. Cover with plastic wrap and chill for 30 minutes. Repeat these steps twice more, giving the dough 2 more single turns.

SHAPING, PROOFING, AND BAKING THE PASTRIES

Grease the molds with butter and sprinkle to coat with sugar so that the pastries caramelize when baking. Place them on a baking sheet. Roll the dough into a 15 × 25-in. (36 × 60-cm) rectangle, about ⅛ in. (4 mm) thick. Cut the rectangle lengthwise into 3 strips 5 in. (12 cm) wide, then widthwise into 5 strips 5 in. (12 cm) wide, to form 15 × 5-in. (12-cm) squares. Fold the four corners of each square in toward the center and place in the molds with the corners facing down. Let proof in a steam oven set to 75°F (24°C), or on a rack in a turned-off oven above a bowl of boiling water, for about 2½ hours. Preheat the oven on fan setting to 325°F (160°C/Gas Mark 3) and bake the pastries for 16–20 minutes until golden brown. As soon as the pastries come out of the oven, turn them out of the molds and let them cool on a rack.

NEW YORK ROLLS

Makes 12

Active time

3 hours

Bulk fermentation time

30 minutes

Resting time

45 minutes–1 hour

Proofing time

1½ hours

Cooking time

12–15 minutes

Storage

Up to 24 hours
in an airtight container

Equipment

Stand mixer + dough hook

Instant-read thermometer

12 × 4-in. (10-cm) cake rings, 1¼ in. (3 cm) deep

Pastry bag with a plain ½-in. (15-mm) tip

Ingredients

Vanilla pastry cream

Scant 1½ cups (350 g/350 ml) whole milk

⅔ cup (150 g/150 ml) heavy cream, min. 35% fat

½ cup (3.5 oz./100 g) sugar, divided

1 vanilla bean, split lengthwise and seeds scraped

1 egg

1 egg yolk

3 tbsp (1 oz./30 g) cornstarch

4 tbsp (2 oz./60 g) butter, diced, at room temperature

Yeasted puff pastry dough

Water dough

2 cups + 2 tbsp (9.5 oz./270 g) cake flour (T45)

½ cup + 2 tsp (135 g/135 ml) whole milk

1 tsp (6 g) salt

0.5 oz. (14 g) fresh yeast

2 tsp (10 g) honey

2½ tbsp (1 oz./30 g) sugar

2 tbsp (1 oz./30 g) butter, diced, at room temperature

Laminating butter

1 stick + 2 tbsp (5 oz./150 g) butter, preferably 84% fat

Dark chocolate ganache

7 oz. (200 g) dark chocolate, 70% cacao

⅔ cup (160 g/160 ml) heavy cream, min. 35% fat

3 tbsp (1.5 oz./40 g) butter, diced, at room temperature

Decoration

Almonds, finely chopped and toasted

PREPARING THE VANILLA PASTRY CREAM
Heat the milk and cream with half the sugar and the vanilla seeds in a saucepan. Meanwhile, whisk together the egg, egg yolk, and remaining sugar in a bowl until pale and thick, then whisk in the cornstarch. Whisking constantly, slowly pour one-third of the hot milk mixture into the egg mixture. Pour the mixture back into the saucepan and bring to a gentle simmer, stirring constantly with a spatula. As soon as the first bubbles appear, remove from the heat. Add the butter and stir until completely smooth. Press plastic wrap over the surface and chill until using.

PREPARING THE YEASTED PUFF PASTRY DOUGH
Knead all the water dough ingredients in the bowl of the stand mixer on low speed for 5 minutes until well combined. Increase the speed to high and knead for 8 minutes until the dough is supple and elastic. The dough temperature should be between 70°F (21°C) and 73°F (23°C). Roll the dough into a 6 × 12-in. (15 × 30-cm) rectangle, cover with plastic wrap, and let ferment for 30 minutes in the refrigerator. Roll the laminating (84%) butter into an 8-in. (20-cm) square (see technique p. 62). Place the butter in the center of the dough and fold the ends of the dough over it to meet in the center, enclosing the butter completely. Roll the dough into an approximate 8 × 20-in. (20 × 50-cm) rectangle. Fold over the shorter ends of the dough so they meet in the center, then fold the dough in half, like a book, to make a double turn. Let rest for 15–30 minutes in the refrigerator. Give the dough a quarter turn clockwise. Roll the dough into an approximate 8 × 20-in. (20 × 50-cm) rectangle, then fold it in 3, like a letter, to make a single turn. Let rest for 30 minutes in the refrigerator.

SHAPING AND PROOFING THE ROLLS
Place the cake rings on a baking sheet lined with parchment paper. Roll the dough into a 12 × 20-in. (30 × 50-cm) rectangle. Trim the edges all around, then roll the dough up from one long side into a tight log. Cut the log into 12 slices, about 1 in. (2.5 cm) thick, and place the slices in the cake rings. Let proof in a steam oven set to 75°F (24°C), or place on a rack in a turned-off oven above a bowl of boiling water, for about 1½ hours.

BAKING THE ROLLS
Preheat the oven to 350°F (180°C/Gas Mark 4) and bake the rolls for 12–15 minutes. Let cool in the cake rings for 10 minutes before removing and placing them on a rack to cool.

PREPARING THE DARK CHOCOLATE GANACHE
Finely chop the chocolate and place it in a heatproof bowl. Bring the cream to a boil in a saucepan, pour it over the chocolate and stir to melt. Add the butter and stir until completely smooth.

DECORATING THE ROLLS
Transfer the vanilla pastry cream to the pastry bag. Once the rolls have cooled completely, pierce the bases with the pastry tip and fill with the cream. Dip the rolls into the chocolate ganache, coating them halfway, and sprinkle with chopped almonds. Let set on a baking sheet lined with parchment paper.

BABKA

Makes 2 babkas, weighing 12.5 oz. (350 g) each

Active time

1½ hours

Bulk fermentation time

1 hour

Resting time

30 minutes

Chilling time

30 minutes

Proofing time

1½ hours

Cooking time

25–30 minutes

Storage

Up to 2 days

Equipment

Stand mixer + dough hook

Instant-read thermometer

2 loaf pans, 7 × 8½ in. (17 × 22 cm), 3 in. (8 cm) deep

Ingredients

Brioche dough

2 cups (9 oz./250 g) all-purpose flour (*gruau*)

⅓ cup (90 g/90 ml) water

¼ cup (2 oz./60 g) lightly beaten egg (about 1¼ eggs)

1 tsp (5 g) salt

0.35 oz. (10 g) fresh yeast

4 tbsp (2.5 oz./65 g) butter, diced, at room temperature, plus extra for greasing

2 tbsp (25 g) sugar

Dark chocolate ganache

3.5 oz. (100 g) dark chocolate, 70% cacao

⅓ cup (80 g/80 ml) heavy cream, min. 35% fat

1 tbsp (20 g) butter, diced, at room temperature

Egg wash

1 egg

1 egg yolk

2 tsp (10 g/10 ml) whole milk

PREPARING THE BRIOCHE DOUGH

Knead all the dough ingredients, except the butter and sugar, in the bowl of the stand mixer on low speed for 5 minutes until well combined. With the mixer running on medium speed, add the butter and sugar and knead until completely incorporated (6–8 minutes). Make sure the dough temperature does not exceed 75°F (24°C). Transfer to a clean bowl, cover with plastic wrap, and let ferment for 1 hour at room temperature. Perform a fold (see technique p. 48), cover the dough with plastic wrap, and let rest in the refrigerator for about 30 minutes.

PREPARING THE DARK CHOCOLATE GANACHE

Finely chop the chocolate and place in a heatproof bowl. Bring the cream to a boil in a saucepan, pour it over the chocolate, and stir to melt. Add the butter and stir until smooth.

SHAPING AND PROOFING THE BABKAS

Roll the dough into a 14 × 16-in. (35 × 40-cm) rectangle, ⅛–¼ in. (3–4 mm) thick, and trim the edges. Chill for 30 minutes, then spread the ganache over the dough in an even layer. Starting with a long side, roll the rectangle into a tight coil. Cut the roll in half lengthwise, then slice each half in two lengthwise down the middle. Make 2 two-strand braids (see technique p. 104) with the cut sides facing upward. Grease the loaf pans with butter and place one braided loaf in each. Place on a baking sheet. Let proof in a steam oven set to 75°F (24°C), or place on a rack in a turned-off oven above a bowl of boiling water, for about 1½ hours.

BAKING THE BABKAS

Preheat the oven to 350°F (180°C/Gas Mark 4). Whisk the egg wash ingredients together. Brush the babkas with the egg wash and bake for 25–30 minutes. Let cool in the pans for 10 minutes before turning out onto a rack to cool completely.

EPIPHANY BRIOCHE

Brioche des rois

Makes 2 brioches, weighing about 10½ oz. (300 g) each

Active time

1½ hours

Bulk fermentation time

1 hour + 10–12 hours in the refrigerator

Proofing time

1½ hours

Cooking time

25 minutes

Storage

Up to 2 days

Equipment

Stand mixer + dough hook

Instant-read thermometer

Ingredients

Brioche dough

2 cups (9 oz./250 g) all-purpose flour (*gruau*)

Scant ¾ cup (5.75 oz./165 g) lightly beaten egg (about 3 eggs)

1 tsp (5 g) salt

0.35 oz. (10 g) fresh yeast

1 stick + 2 tbsp (5 oz./140 g) butter, diced, at room temperature

2½ tbsp (1 oz./30 g) sugar

1–2 tsp (5–10 g/5–10 ml) orange-flower water

Egg wash

1 egg

1 egg yolk

2 tsp (10 g/10 ml) whole milk

Syrup

1 cup (250 g/250 ml) water

⅔ cup (4.5 oz./125 g) sugar

Decoration

5.75 oz. (160 g) candied fruits of your choice

Pearl sugar

PREPARING THE BRIOCHE DOUGH (1 DAY AHEAD)

Knead all the dough ingredients, except the butter, sugar, and orange-flower water, in the bowl of the stand mixer on low speed for 5 minutes until well combined. Increase the speed to medium and knead for 6–8 minutes until the dough is supple and elastic. With the mixer running on medium speed, add the butter, sugar, and orange-flower water, and knead until completely incorporated (6–8 minutes). Make sure the dough temperature does not exceed 75°F (24°C). Place in a clean bowl, cover with plastic wrap, and let ferment for 1 hour at room temperature, folding it once (see technique p. 48) halfway through the fermentation time. Shape the dough into a ball, return it to the bowl, and cover with plastic wrap. Let rest in the refrigerator for 10–12 hours.

SHAPING AND PROOFING THE BRIOCHE RINGS

The next day, divide the dough into 2 pieces, about 5.25 oz. (150 g) each. Shape each piece into a baguette-like log, 22 in. (55 cm) long. Join the ends of each log together to make 2 rings. Place on baking sheets lined with parchment paper. Whisk together the egg wash ingredients and brush over the dough rings. Let proof in a steam oven set to 75°F (24°C), or place on a rack in a turned-off oven above a bowl of boiling water, for about 1½ hours.

PREPARING THE SYRUP

Combine the water and sugar in a saucepan and bring to a boil, stirring to dissolve the sugar. Let cool before using.

BAKING THE BRIOCHE RINGS

Preheat the oven to 350°F (180°C/Gas Mark 4). Brush the rings again with egg wash and bake for about 25 minutes. As soon as the rings come out of the oven, brush them with the syrup and arrange the dried fruit attractively on top. Coat the sides with pearl sugar and let cool on a rack.

INDIVIDUAL PINK PRALINE BRIOCHES

Briochettes aux pralines roses

Makes 10

Active time
1½ hours

Bulk fermentation time
30 minutes + overnight

Proofing time
1½ hours

Cooking time
20 minutes

Storage
Up to 24 hours in an airtight container

Equipment
Stand mixer + dough hook
Instant-read thermometer
10 × 3-in. (8-cm) muffin pans, 1½ in. (4 cm) deep

Ingredients

Brioche dough
1 cup (4.25 oz./125 g) all-purpose flour (*gruau*)
1 cup (4.25 oz./125 g) white bread flour (T65)
⅔ cup (5.25 oz./150 g) lightly beaten egg (3 eggs), well chilled
2½ tsp (10 g) superfine sugar
0.35 oz. (10 g) fresh yeast
1 tsp (5 g) salt
1 stick plus 2 tsp (4.5 oz./125 g) butter, diced, at room temperature

Butter for the pans

Pink pralines
1 lb. (440 g) pink pralines (*pralines roses*), broken into rough pieces

Egg wash
1 egg

PREPARING THE DOUGH (1 DAY AHEAD)

Knead all the dough ingredients, except the butter, in the bowl of the stand mixer on low speed for 5 minutes until well combined. Increase the speed to high and knead for 5 minutes until the dough is supple and elastic. With the mixer running on low speed, add the butter and knead for 5 minutes until completely incorporated. Make sure the dough temperature does not exceed 77°F–79°F (25°C–26°C). Place in a clean bowl, cover with plastic wrap, and let ferment for 30 minutes at room temperature. Fold the dough once (see technique p. 48), cover again with plastic wrap, and let ferment overnight in the refrigerator.

SHAPING AND PROOFING THE DOUGH

The next day, grease the muffin pans with butter and place on a baking sheet. Divide the dough into 10 pieces, weighing 1.75 oz. (55 g) each, and roll into 2 × 6-in. (5 × 15-cm) rectangles. Place about 1 oz. (25 g) pink pralines on one of the dough rectangles and fold it in 3, like a letter, as if giving the dough a single turn. Rotate the dough 90° clockwise, then gently roll it into a 2 × 6-in. (5 × 15-cm) rectangle again. Top with 0.5 oz. (15 g) pralines, fold in 3, and shape into a ball. Repeat with the other dough pieces and place them in the molds. Let proof for 1½ hours at room temperature in a draft-free place.

BAKING THE BRIOCHES

Preheat the oven to 285°F (140°C/Gas Mark 1) on fan setting. The temperature is low to prevent the pralines from caramelizing. Lightly beat the egg and brush it over the brioches. Bake for about 20 minutes until lightly golden. Let them cool in the pans before turning out.

GÂCHE BRIOCHE

Makes 2 brioches to serve 6

Active time
45 minutes

Pre-ferment fermentation time
3 hours

Bulk fermentation time
1 hour + overnight in the refrigerator

Chilling time
30 minutes

Proofing time
1½ hours

Cooking time
20–30 minutes

Storage
Up to 2 days

Equipment
Stand mixer + dough hook
Instant-read thermometer
Bread lame

Ingredients

Pre-ferment
1⅔ cups (7 oz./200 g) all-purpose flour (T55)
½ cup (125 g/125 ml) whole milk, well chilled
0.25 oz. (8 g) fresh yeast, crumbled

Brioche dough
Pre-ferment (see above)
1⅔ cups (7 oz./200 g) all-purpose flour (T55)
Scant ½ cup (3.5 oz./100 g) lightly beaten egg (2 eggs)
Scant ½ cup (3.5 oz./100 g) crème fraîche
0.5 oz. (12 g) fresh yeast
2 tsp (10 g) salt
5 tsp (20 g/20 ml) rum
1 stick + 2 tsp (4.5 oz./125 g) butter, diced, at room temperature
⅓ cup (2.75 oz./75 g) sugar

Egg wash
1 egg
1 egg yolk
2 tsp (10 g/10 ml) whole milk

PREPARING THE PRE-FERMENT (1 DAY AHEAD)
Whisk together the flour, milk, and yeast in a bowl until smooth. Cover with plastic wrap and let ferment for 3 hours at room temperature.

PREPARING THE BRIOCHE DOUGH (1 DAY AHEAD)
Knead all the dough ingredients, except the butter and sugar, in the bowl of the stand mixer on low speed for 5 minutes until well combined. Increase the speed to medium and knead for 6–8 minutes until the dough is supple and elastic. With the mixer running on medium speed, add the butter and sugar and knead until completely incorporated (6–8 minutes). Make sure the dough temperature does not exceed 75°F (24°C). Place in a clean bowl, cover with plastic wrap, and let ferment for 1 hour at room temperature. Fold the dough once (see technique p. 48), return it to the bowl, and cover with plastic wrap. Let rest in the refrigerator overnight.

SHAPING AND PROOFING THE BRIOCHES
The next day, divide the dough into 2 pieces. Shape into balls and chill for 30 minutes. Shape each ball into a *bâtard* (see technique p. 51) and place on a baking sheet lined with parchment paper. Whisk together the egg wash ingredients and brush over the brioches. Let proof in a steam oven set to 75°F (24°C), or place on a rack in a turned-off oven above a bowl of boiling water, for about 1½ hours.

BAKING THE BRIOCHES
Preheat the oven to 350°F (180°C/Gas Mark 4). Using the bread lame, slash each brioche lengthwise down the center. Bake for 20–30 minutes until golden brown. Immediately transfer to a rack and let cool at room temperature.

BRAIDED VENDÉE BRIOCHE

Brioche vendéenne

Makes 2 brioches to serve 6–8

Active time

1 hour

***Pâte fermentée* fermentation time**

Overnight

Bulk fermentation time

1 hour + overnight in the refrigerator

Proofing time

1½ hours

Cooking time

20–30 minutes

Storage

Up to 2 days

Equipment

Stand mixer + dough hook

Instant-read thermometer

Ingredients

Pâte fermentée

⅔ cup + 1 tbsp (3 oz./90 g) white bread flour (T65)

Scant ¼ cup (56 g/56 ml) water

¼ tsp (1.5 g) salt

0.05 oz. (1.5 g) fresh yeast

Brioche dough

5.25 oz. (150 g) *pâte fermentée* (see above)

Scant 4½ cups (1 lb. 2 oz./500 g) all-purpose flour (T55)

1 cup (8.75 oz./250 g) lightly beaten egg (5 eggs)

⅓ cup (80 g/80 ml) whole milk

0.75 oz. (20 g) fresh yeast

2 tsp (10 g) salt

1 stick + 2 tbsp (5.25 oz./150 g) butter, diced, at room temperature

Scant ⅓ cup (2 oz./60 g) sugar

2 tsp (10 g/10 ml) rum

1 tsp (5 g/5 ml) orange-flower water

1 tsp (5 g) vanilla powder

Egg wash

1 egg

1 egg yolk

2 tsp (10 g/10 ml) whole milk

Decoration

Pearl sugar

PREPARING THE PÂTE FERMENTÉE (2 DAYS AHEAD)

Mix the flour, water, salt, and yeast together in the bowl of the stand mixer and knead on low speed, or by hand, for 10 minutes, until smooth. Place in a bowl, cover with plastic wrap, and let ferment overnight in the refrigerator.

PREPARING THE BRIOCHE DOUGH (1 DAY AHEAD)

Knead all the dough ingredients, except the butter, sugar, and aromatics (rum, orange-flower water, and vanilla powder) in the bowl of the stand mixer on low speed for 5 minutes until well combined. Increase the speed to medium and knead for 6–8 minutes until the dough is supple and elastic. With the mixer running on medium speed, add the butter and sugar and knead for 6–8 minutes until incorporated. Add the aromatics and continue to knead for 1–2 minutes. Make sure the dough temperature does not exceed 75°F (24°C). Place in a clean bowl, cover with plastic wrap, and let ferment for 1 hour at room temperature. Fold the dough once (see technique p. 48), return it to the bowl, and cover with plastic wrap. Let rest in the refrigerator overnight.

SHAPING AND PROOFING THE BRAIDED BRIOCHES

The next day, divide the dough into 6 pieces. Shape each piece into a 20-in. (50-cm) strand, then make 2 three-strand braids (see technique p. 106). Place on a baking sheet lined with parchment paper. Whisk the egg wash ingredients together and brush over the braids. Let proof in a steam oven set to 75°F (24°C), or place on a rack in a turned-off oven above a bowl of boiling water, for about 1½ hours.

BAKING THE BRAIDED BRIOCHES

Preheat the oven to 350°F (180°C/Gas Mark 4). Brush the brioches again with egg wash and sprinkle with pearl sugar. Bake for 20–30 minutes until golden brown. Immediately transfer to a rack and let cool at room temperature.

VEGAN BRIOCHE

Brioche vegan

Makes 5 brioches, weighing about 4.25 oz. (120 g) each

Active time
45 minutes

Resting time
At least 1 hour,
or preferably overnight,
+ 30 minutes

Bulk fermentation time
30 minutes

Chilling time
At least 1 hour,
or preferably overnight

Proofing time
1½ hours

Cooking time
20 minutes

Storage
Up to 2 days
in a well-sealed paper bag or well wrapped in a clean dish towel

Equipment

Stand mixer + paddle beater

5 nonstick loaf pans, 3 × 7 in. (8 × 18 cm), 3 in. (8 cm) deep

Ingredients

Vegan brioche dough

⅓ cup (75 g/75 ml) soy milk, divided

Scant ⅔ cup (1.75 oz./50 g) chickpea flour

⅓ cup (2.5 oz./75 g) pumpkin purée

1 banana, mashed

1⅔ cups (7 oz./200 g) all-purpose flour (*gruau*)

0.35 oz. (10 g) fresh yeast, crumbled

1 tsp (5 g) salt

2½ tbsp (1 oz./30 g) sugar

Scant ½ cup (105 g/120 ml) neutral vegetable oil

A little soy milk for brushing

Vegan crumb topping

Generous 2 tbsp (1 oz./30 g) brown sugar

⅓ cup (1.5 oz./40 g) whole wheat flour

2 tbsp (1 oz./30 g) margarine, well chilled and diced

Scant ¼ cup (20 g) almond flour

Scant ¼ tsp (1 g) salt

Ground cinnamon to taste

PREPARING THE BRIOCHE DOUGH

In a saucepan, bring 3½ tbsp (50 g/50 ml) of the soy milk to a boil. Stirring, pour the soy milk over the chickpea flour in a bowl. Stir until smooth. Cover the bowl with plastic wrap and let rest for at least 1 hour, or preferably overnight, in the refrigerator. Place the pumpkin purée and mashed banana in the bowl of the stand mixer. Add the chilled chickpea flour-soy milk paste, then add the all-purpose flour, remaining soy milk, and yeast. Knead on low speed until well combined and completely smooth (this could take up to about 30 minutes). Add the salt and sugar and knead for a few minutes until dissolved and well distributed. Pour in the oil in 6 equal quantities, kneading after each addition until the dough has completely absorbed it. Cover the bowl with plastic wrap and let ferment for 30 minutes at room temperature. Gently fold the dough (see technique p. 48), cover with plastic wrap, and chill for at least 1 hour, or overnight.

SHAPING THE DOUGH

Divide the dough into 30 pieces weighing 0.75 oz. (20 g) each and roll them into balls. Cover with plastic wrap and let rest for 30 minutes in the refrigerator. Roll into smooth balls again, then place 6 in each pan in a staggered pattern. Let proof in a steam oven set to 77°F (25°C), or on a rack in a turned-off oven above a bowl of boiling water, for 1½ hours.

PREPARING THE VEGAN CRUMB TOPPING AND BAKING THE BRIOCHES

Preheat the oven to 325°F (160°C/Gas Mark 3). Chill the proofed brioches in the refrigerator for 5 minutes, then brush with soy milk. Combine the crumb topping ingredients using your fingertips until the mixture resembles coarse crumbs. Take care not to overmix, to avoid turning the crumbs into a paste. Sprinkle the topping over the brioches and press down gently to make it stick. Bake for about 20 minutes until golden. Immediately turn the loaves out of the pans and let them cool completely on a rack.

CHEFS' NOTES

• When starch comes into contact with a hot liquid, it gelatinizes. Using gelatinized starch in this recipe locks moisture in the dough. This makes the brioche more moist and spongy, and compensates for the absence of animal fats and eggs.

• It can take a while to make this dough smooth, but mixing on low speed prevents it from getting too hot.

KOUGELHOPF

Kouglof

Makes 2 kougelhopfs to serve 6–8

Active time

1 hour

Pre-ferment fermentation time

3 hours

Bulk fermentation time

1 hour + overnight in the refrigerator

Chilling time

30 minutes

Proofing time

1½ hours

Cooking time

30–35 minutes

Storage

Up to 2 days

Equipment

Stand mixer + dough hook

Instant-read thermometer

2 × 8-in. (20-cm) silicone kougelhopf molds

Ingredients

Pre-ferment

¾ cup + 2 tbsp (3.5 oz./100 g) all-purpose flour (T55)

¼ cup (60 g/60 ml) whole milk, well chilled

0.25 oz. (8 g) fresh yeast, crumbled

Kougelhopf dough

Pre-ferment (see above)

3¼ cups (14 oz./400 g) all-purpose flour (T55)

Scant ½ cup (3.5 oz./100 g) lightly beaten egg (2 eggs)

½ cup minus 1 tbsp (110 g/110 ml) whole milk

0.5 oz. (12 g) fresh yeast

2 tsp (10 g) salt

7 tbsp (3.5 oz./100 g) butter, diced, at room temperature

½ cup minus 1½ tbsp (2.75 oz./80 g) sugar

To bake and serve

Butter for the molds

2 tbsp (20 g) whole almonds

Confectioners' sugar

PREPARING THE PRE-FERMENT (1 DAY AHEAD)

Whisk together the flour, milk, and yeast in a bowl until smooth. Cover with plastic wrap and let ferment for 3 hours at room temperature.

PREPARING THE KOUGELHOPF DOUGH (1 DAY AHEAD)

Knead all the dough ingredients, except the butter and sugar, in the bowl of the stand mixer on low speed for 5 minutes until well combined. Increase the speed to medium and knead for 6–8 minutes until the dough is supple and elastic. With the mixer running on medium speed, add the butter and sugar and knead until completely incorporated (6–8 minutes). Make sure the dough temperature does not exceed 75°F (24°C). Place in a clean bowl, cover with plastic wrap, and let ferment for 1 hour at room temperature. Fold the dough once (see technique p. 48), return it to the bowl, and cover with plastic wrap. Let rest in the refrigerator overnight.

SHAPING AND PROOFING THE KOUGELHOPFS

The next day, divide the dough into 2 pieces. Shape into balls and chill for 30 minutes. Grease the molds with a little butter and arrange the almonds around the base of each, placing them in the grooves. Shape each dough ball into a small ring by making a hole in the center (see technique p. 98). Transfer the dough to the molds, taking care not to displace the almonds. Let proof in a steam oven set to 75°F (24°C), or place on a rack in a turned-off oven above a bowl of boiling water, for about 1½ hours.

BAKING THE KOUGELHOPFS

Preheat the oven to 350°F (180°C/Gas Mark 4) and bake the kougelhopfs for 30–35 minutes. Turn them carefully out of the molds onto a rack to cool. Once they have cooled completely, dust the tops with confectioners' sugar.

PANETTONE

Makes 2 panettones, weighing 1 lb. (450 g) each

Active time

2 hours

Maceration time

4 hours

Soaking time

30 minutes

Levain fermentation time

3 hours

Bulk fermentation time

2 hours

Proofing time

3 hours

Cooking time

35 minutes

Cooling time

40 minutes

Storage

Up to 1 week well covered in plastic wrap

Equipment

Stand mixer + dough hook

Instant-read thermometer

Bowl scraper

2 × 5½-in. (14-cm) paper panettone molds, 5 in. (12 cm) deep

Pastry bag with a plain round tip

4 metal or wooden skewers

Ingredients

Macerated dried fruit and nuts

½ cup (2.5 oz./70 g) raisins

½ cup (2.5 oz./70 g) hazelnuts, chopped

½ cup (2.5 oz./70 g) dried cranberries

2½ tbsp (40 g/40 ml) rum

Levain bath

3.25 oz. (90 g) ripe stiff levain (see technique p. 38)

¾ tsp (3 g) superfine sugar

Scant 1 cup (230 g/230 ml) water at 100°F (38°C)

Refreshed levain

2.5 oz. (75 g) "washed" levain (see above)

⅔ cup (2.5 oz./75 g) all-purpose flour (*gruau*)

2 tbsp + 1 tsp (35 g/35 ml) whole milk at 86°F (30°C)

Panettone dough

6.5 oz. (185 g) refreshed levain (see above)

½ tsp (3 g) salt

0.15 oz. (4 g) fresh yeast

Scant ½ cup (4.25 oz./120 g) egg yolk (about 6 yolks)

Scant ½ cup (2.75 oz./80 g) superfine sugar, divided

1 cup + scant ½ cup (6 oz./175 g) all-purpose flour (*gruau*)

1 stick (4 oz./115 g) butter, diced, at room temperature

⅔ cup (5.25 oz./150 g) lightly beaten egg (3 eggs), well chilled (for *bassinage*)

Macerated fruit and nuts (see left), drained

Neutral oil and butter for greasing

Almond glaze

Scant 1 cup (3.25 oz./90 g) almond flour

Scant ⅓ cup (2 oz./60 g) superfine sugar

¼ cup (2 oz./60 g) egg white (about 2 whites)

Decoration

Sliced almonds

Confectioners' sugar

MACERATING THE DRIED FRUIT AND NUTS

Place the raisins, hazelnuts, and cranberries in a bowl with the rum and let macerate for 4 hours.

"BATHING" THE LEVAIN

Cut the stiff levain into ¾-in. (2-cm) dice. In a bowl large enough to hold the levain, stir the sugar into the water until dissolved. Add the diced levain and let soak for 30 minutes. This "bath", known as *bagnetto* in Italian, balances the acidity and gives the levain a milder taste.

REFRESHING THE LEVAIN

Knead all the ingredients in the bowl of the stand mixer on low speed for 5 minutes, adding a little more milk if the levain is too stiff and won't come together. Turn the levain out onto a work surface, then roll it out and fold it several times to make it smooth, rotating it 90° clockwise each time. Roll the levain out again, place it on a sheet of plastic wrap greased with a little neutral oil or butter, and roll it up very tightly. Let ferment in a steam oven set to 75°F (24°C), or on a rack in a turned-off oven above a bowl of boiling water, for 3 hours.

PREPARING THE PANETTONE DOUGH

Knead the levain, salt, yeast, egg yolk, and half the sugar in the bowl of the stand mixer on low speed until the salt, sugar, and yeast are dissolved and the levain diluted. Add the flour and knead on low speed until well combined, then increase the speed to high and knead until the dough is completely smooth (even when smooth, this dough will still stick to the sides of the bowl). Add the remaining sugar and knead until smooth again, then add the butter and knead until the butter is incorporated and the dough completely smooth. With the mixer running on low speed, gradually add the egg in 5 equal quantities, as needed, depending on the consistency of the dough, which should be smooth, very supple, and sticky (*bassinage*). Add the macerated fruit and nuts and knead until well distributed. Make sure the dough temperature does not exceed 79°F–81°F (26°C–27°C). Place the dough in a large bowl and cover with plastic wrap. Let ferment for 1 hour in a steam oven set to 75°F (24°C), or on a rack in a turned-off oven above a bowl of boiling water. After 1 hour, give the dough one fold (see technique p. 48), then cover the bowl again with plastic wrap and return it to the steam oven set to 75°F (24°C) or a turned-off oven above a bowl of boiling water. Let ferment for an additional 1 hour.

SHAPING AND PROOFING THE PANETTONES

Divide the dough into 2 pieces weighing 1 lb. (450 g) each and place on a work surface lightly greased with butter. Shape each piece into a tight ball by tucking the bowl scraper underneath as you rotate the dough against the work surface. Place in the panettone molds on a baking sheet. Let proof in a steam oven set to 75°F (24°C), or on a rack in a turned-off oven above a bowl of boiling water, for about 3 hours. The dough should rise to the tops of the molds or slightly above them.

PREPARING THE ALMOND GLAZE

Stir together all the ingredients until well combined and transfer to the pastry bag.

BAKING THE PANETTONES

Preheat the oven to 300°F (150°C/Gas Mark 2) on fan setting. Pipe the almond glaze evenly over the tops of the panettones, then sprinkle with sliced almonds and dust with confectioners' sugar. Bake for about 35 minutes until uniformly golden. Panettone is very fragile right after baking and can easily collapse. To avoid this, pierce all the way through the panettones from side to side with two skewers, just above the base, hang them upside down, and let cool for 40 minutes.

CHOCOLATE CHIP VIENNA BREAD

Viennoise aux pépites de chocolat

Makes 6 small baguettes, weighing about 6.75 oz. (190 g) each

Active time
1 hour

Bulk fermentation time
45 minutes–1 hour

Resting time
15 minutes

Proofing time
1¼–1½ hours

Cooking time
12–15 minutes

Storage
Up to 2 days

Equipment
Stand mixer + dough hook
Instant-read thermometer
Baguette pans for 6 half-baguettes
Bread lame

Ingredients
2.75 oz. (80 g) *pâte fermentée* (see recipe p. 142)
3¼ cups (14 oz./400 g) white bread flour (T65)
¾ cup + 2 tbsp (3.5 oz./100 g) all-purpose flour (*gruau*)
1 egg
Scant 1 cup (230 g/230 ml) water
¼ cup (25 g) milk powder
2½ tbsp (1 oz./30 g) sugar
1 oz. (25 g) fresh yeast
2 tsp (10 g) salt
3 tbsp (1.5 oz./40 g) butter, diced, at room temperature
Scant 1 cup (5.25 oz./150 g) chocolate chips

Egg wash
1 egg
1 egg yolk
2 tsp (10 g/10 ml) whole milk

PREPARING THE DOUGH
Knead all the ingredients, except the butter and chocolate chips, in the bowl of the stand mixer on low speed for 4 minutes until well combined. Increase the speed to high and knead for 4 minutes until the dough is supple and elastic. With the mixer running on low speed, add the butter and knead until completely incorporated (6–8 minutes). Add the chocolate chips and knead for a few seconds until evenly distributed. Make sure the dough temperature does not exceed 75°F (24°C). Place the dough in a clean bowl, cover with plastic wrap, and let ferment for 45 minutes–1 hour at room temperature.

SHAPING AND PROOFING THE BAGUETTES
Divide the dough into 6 pieces weighing about 6.75 oz. (190 g) each. Shape into small baguettes (see technique p. 51) and place in the baguette pans. Let rest for 15 minutes. Whisk the egg wash ingredients together and brush over the baguettes, then score with diagonal slashes using the bread lame (see technique p. 57). Let proof in a steam oven set to 75°F (24°C), or place on a rack in a turned-off oven above a bowl of boiling water, for 1¼–1½ hours.

BAKING THE BAGUETTES
Preheat the oven to 425°F (220°C/Gas Mark 7). Brush the baguettes again with egg wash and bake for 12–15 minutes. Immediately remove the baguettes from the pans, place on a rack, and let cool at room temperature.

CARDAMOM BRIOCHE BUNS

Brioche à la cardamome

Makes 2 brioches, each to serve 4

Active time
2 hours

Fermentation time
3 hours

Bulk fermentation time
2 hours

Resting time
30 minutes

Proofing time
1½ hours

Cooking time
20 minutes

Storage
Up to 1 week well covered in plastic wrap

Equipment
Stand mixer + whisk and dough hook
Instant-read thermometer

Ingredients

Milk levain
- 1 oz. (25 g) ripe liquid levain (see technique p. 40)
- 2 tbsp (30 g/30 ml) whole milk at 113°F (45°C)
- ⅔ cup (2.5 oz./75 g) white bread flour (T65)

Brioche dough
- Milk levain (see above)
- 2 cups (9 oz./250 g) white bread flour (T65)
- Scant ½ cup (3.5 oz./100 g) lightly beaten egg (2 eggs), well chilled
- 3½ tbsp (50 g/50 ml) whole milk, well chilled
- 1 tsp (6 g) salt
- Scant ⅓ cup (2 oz./60 g) superfine sugar, divided
- 7 tbsp (3.5 oz./100 g) butter, diced, at room temperature

Cardamom butter
- 7 tbsp (3.5 oz./100 g) butter, softened
- ½ cup (3.5 oz./100 g) brown sugar
- 2 tbsp (16 g) ground cardamom

CHEFS' NOTES

Milk levain combines the advantages of stiff and liquid levains. It has the texture of stiff levain, which gives the dough significant strength, and the rich milky notes of liquid levain.

PREPARING THE MILK LEVAIN

Whisk the levain and warm milk vigorously in the bowl of the stand mixer to aerate the levain and make it frothy. Change the whisk for the dough hook attachment, add the flour, and knead on low speed for 5 minutes until well combined. Shape the dough into a very tight ball and cut a cross on the top. Place in a clean bowl, cover with plastic wrap, and let ferment in a steam oven set to 95°F (35°C), or place on a rack in a turned-off oven above a bowl of boiling water, for 3 hours.

PREPARING THE BRIOCHE DOUGH

Knead the milk levain, flour, egg, milk, salt, and half the sugar in the bowl of the stand mixer on low speed for 5 minutes until well combined. Increase the speed to high and knead until supple and elastic. With the mixer running on low speed, knead in the remaining sugar, then add the butter and knead until the dough is completely smooth. Make sure the dough temperature does not exceed 77°F (25°C). Place in a clean bowl, cover with plastic wrap, and let ferment for 1 hour at room temperature. Fold the dough (see technique p. 48), cover again with plastic wrap, and let ferment for an additional 1 hour. Divide the dough into 8 pieces weighing 3.25 oz. (90 g) each, and gently shape each one into a ball. Cover with plastic wrap and let rest for 30 minutes at room temperature.

PREPARING THE CARDAMOM BUTTER

Place the butter, brown sugar, and ground cardamom in a bowl and stir until well blended. Set aside at room temperature until using. (Do not chill, as it will be too difficult to spread.)

SHAPING THE BUNS

Roll each piece of dough into a 7-in. (18-cm) disk (if the dough sticks or resists, place it in the refrigerator for a few minutes). Brush a little water around the edges of 6 disks of dough to moisten. Divide the cardamom butter between these 6 disks and spread into an even layer. Stack 3 cardamom butter-covered disks one on top of the other, and place one of the plain disks on top. Do the same with the remaining dough disks. Cut each stack into 12 equal parts resembling flower petals, leaving a ¾-in. (2-cm) uncut section in the center. In each "petal," make a cut lengthways down the center, leaving a border of about 1⁄16–⅛ in. (2–3 mm) at the outer edge. To make the layers visible, turn them to face upward and bring them together. Place the buns on a baking sheet lined with parchment paper and let proof in a steam oven set to (75°F/24°C), or on a rack in a turned-off oven above a bowl of boiling water, for 1½ hours.

BAKING THE BUNS

Preheat the oven to 300°F (150°C/Gas Mark 2) and bake the buns for 20 minutes.

HAZELNUT AND CHOCOLATE PUFF PASTRIES

Écrin feuilleté aux noisettes

Makes 8

Active time

3 hours

Bulk fermentation time

15 minutes

Freezing time

1¾ hours

Proofing time

1½ hours

Cooking time

20 minutes

Storage

Up to several days in an airtight container

Equipment

Stand mixer + dough hook

Instant-read thermometer

Pastry bag with a plain round tip

8 × 4-in. (10-cm) baking rings, ¾ in. (2 cm) deep

5-in. (12-cm) round cookie cutter

4-in. (10-cm) round cookie cutter

Ingredients

Yeasted puff pastry dough

Plain base dough

2 cups (9 oz./250 g) all-purpose flour (*gruau*)

2 cups (9 oz./250 g) white bread flour (T65)

1 cup + 5 tsp (270 g/270 ml) whole milk, well chilled

2 tbsp (25 g) butter, diced, at room temperature

Scant ⅓ cup (2 oz./60 g) superfine sugar

0.75 oz. (20 g) fresh yeast

2 tsp (10 g) salt

Hazelnut base dough

8 oz. (225 g) plain base dough (see left)

Scant 1 tbsp (10 g) hazelnut paste

1¼ tsp (3 g) unsweetened cocoa powder

Chocolate base dough

8 oz. (225 g) plain base dough (see left)

2 tbsp + ½ tsp (15 g) unsweetened cocoa powder

2 tsp (10 g) butter, at room temperature

2 tsp (10 g) whole milk, well chilled

Laminating butter

2⅔ sticks (10½ oz./300 g) butter, preferably 84% fat

Hazelnut financier batter

4 tbsp (1.75 oz./55 g) butter

½ cup (1.75 oz./50 g) hazelnut flour

¼ cup (1.5 oz./35 g) white bread flour (T65)

Scant ⅔ cup (2.75 oz./80 g) confectioners' sugar

Scant ⅓ cup (2.25 oz./65 g) egg white (about 2 whites)

Dark chocolate ganache with cacao nibs

5.25 oz. (150 g) dark chocolate, 70% cacao

⅓ cup (95 g/95 ml) heavy cream, min. 35% fat

1.5 oz. (40 g) cacao nibs

Syrup

¼ cup (60 g/60 ml) water

Scant ½ cup (3¼ oz./90 g) sugar

PREPARING THE PLAIN, HAZELNUT, AND CHOCOLATE BASE DOUGHS

Knead all the plain base dough ingredients in the bowl of the stand mixer on low speed for 5 minutes until well combined. Increase the speed to high and knead for 5 minutes until the dough is supple and elastic. Make sure the dough temperature does not exceed 70°F–73°F (21°C–23°C) for any of the base doughs. Divide the dough into 4 pieces weighing 8 oz. (225 g) each and set 2 aside (these will remain plain). To prepare the hazelnut base dough, knead the plain base dough, hazelnut paste, and cocoa powder in the bowl of the stand mixer on medium speed until well blended and smooth. Remove from the bowl. To prepare the chocolate base dough, knead the plain base dough, cocoa powder, butter, and milk in the bowl of the stand mixer on medium speed until well blended and smooth. Gently flatten the 4 pieces of dough into ovals, then fold the top and bottom edges toward the center and turn the pieces over. Cover with plastic wrap and let ferment for 15 minutes at room temperature. Roll each piece of dough into a 4 × 8-in. (10 × 20-cm) rectangle with a thickness of 1/4 in. (5 mm), cover with plastic wrap, and freeze for 30 minutes.

LAMINATING THE PUFF PASTRY DOUGH

Divide the 84% butter into 4 pieces weighing 2.5 oz. (75 g) each. Roll each piece into a 4-in. (10-cm) square (see technique p. 62). Freeze for 15 minutes. Working with one piece of dough at a time, place a square of butter in the center and fold the dough over to enclose the butter completely, obtaining a square. Dust the work surface very lightly with flour and roll the dough into a 4 × 16-in. (10 × 40-cm) rectangle. To give the dough a single turn, fold the bottom third of the dough upward, then fold the top third down over it (see technique p. 64). Cover the dough with plastic wrap and let rest for 15 minutes in the freezer. Repeat these steps once more to give the dough another single turn. Do the same with all 4 pieces of dough, making sure they are all the same length. Cover with plastic wrap and let rest for 30 minutes in the freezer.

PREPARING THE HAZELNUT FINANCIER BATTER

Make browned butter (*beurre noisette*) by heating the butter in a saucepan beyond the melting point until it turns golden brown and has a slightly nutty aroma. Remove from the heat and let cool. Mix together the hazelnut flour, bread flour, and confectioners' sugar in a bowl, then gradually whisk in the egg white. Pour in the cooled browned butter and stir until well blended. Transfer to the pastry bag.

PREPARING THE DARK CHOCOLATE GANACHE WITH CACAO NIBS

Finely chop the chocolate and place it in a heatproof bowl. Bring the cream to a boil in a saucepan, pour it over the chocolate, and stir to melt. Stir in the cacao nibs.

SHAPING THE PUFF PASTRY LAYERS

Grease the baking rings with butter and place on a baking sheet lined with parchment paper. Roll one of the pieces of plain yeasted puff pastry dough into a 4 × 16-in. (10 × 40-cm) rectangle with a thickness of 1/6 in. (4 mm) and lightly moisten the surface with water. Roll the other pieces to the same dimensions and thickness and cut each one crosswise into strips 1/2 in. (1 cm) wide. Moisten the strips and, alternating the colors, stick them together, one on top of the other, then place on the plain pastry rectangle with the cut sides facing up so the puff pastry layers are visible. Roll out together to a thickness of about 1/10 in. (2.5 mm) to obtain a 16 × 24-in. (40 × 60-cm) rectangle. Cut out 8 disks of the multicolored dough using the 5-in. (12-cm) cutter. Line the base and sides of the baking rings with the disks; the dough should come about halfway up the sides of the rings. Set the remaining dough aside for the tops.

ASSEMBLING THE PASTRIES

Fill each base with 1.25 oz. (35 g) ganache and 1.25 oz. (35 g) financier batter, spreading each one into an even layer. Cut out 8 disks of multicolored dough using the 4-in. (10-cm) cutter and cover the pastries with them. Let proof for 1½ hours at room temperature in a draft-free place.

PREPARING THE SYRUP

Combine the water and sugar in a saucepan and bring to a boil, stirring until the sugar dissolves. Set aside at room temperature.

BAKING THE PASTRIES

Preheat the oven to 325°F (160°C/Gas Mark 3) on fan setting. Cover the rings with a sheet of parchment paper and place a baking sheet on top to keep the pastry flat during baking. Bake for 20 minutes. As soon as the pastries are taken out of the oven, carefully remove the baking rings and brush the pastries with a little syrup.

PROVENÇAL OLIVE OIL BRIOCHE

Pompe à huile

Makes 3 brioches, weighing about 11.25 oz. (320 g) each

Active time

1 hour

Bulk fermentation time

2 hours + 10–12 hours in the refrigerator

Resting time

30 minutes

Proofing time

1 hour

Cooking time

18–20 minutes

Storage

Up to 24 hours

Equipment

Stand mixer + dough hook

Instant-read thermometer

Bench scraper

Ingredients

4 cups + 2 tbsp (1 lb. 2 oz./500 g) all-purpose flour (T55)

1 cup minus 3 tbsp (200 g/200 ml) water

1¾ tsp (9 g) salt

0.75 oz. (20 g) fresh yeast

3 tbsp (40 g/44 ml) olive oil

2 tbsp + 1 tsp (35 g/35 ml) orange juice

1 tbsp (15 g/15 ml) lemon juice

⅓ cup (2.75 oz./75 g) lightly beaten egg (about 1½ eggs)

Scant 1 tsp (3 g) green aniseed

Finely grated zest of 1 lemon

Finely grated zest of 1 orange

3 tbsp (40 g/44 ml) olive oil (for *bassinage*)

To finish

Olive oil

PREPARING THE DOUGH (1 DAY AHEAD)

Knead all the ingredients, except the 3 tbsp (40 g/44 ml) olive oil for the *bassinage* stage, in the bowl of the stand mixer on low speed for 3 minutes until well combined. Increase the speed to medium and knead for 10 minutes until the dough is supple. Gradually add the 3 tbsp (40 g/44 ml) olive oil as needed, depending on the consistency of the dough, which should be supple (*bassinage*). Make sure the dough temperature does not exceed 77°F (25°C). Place in a clean bowl, cover with plastic wrap, and let ferment for 2 hours at room temperature, folding the dough once after 1 hour (see technique p. 48). After 2 hours at room temperature, shape the dough into a ball, return it to the bowl, and cover with plastic wrap. Let ferment for 10–12 hours in the refrigerator.

SHAPING AND PROOFING THE DOUGH

The next day, divide the dough into 3 pieces weighing 11.25 oz. (320 g) each. Shape into balls and let rest for 30 minutes. Shape each ball into a 12-in. (30-cm) disk, ¼ in. (5 mm) thick, and place on a baking sheet lined with parchment paper. Using the bench scraper, make 8 slits in each one, radiating out from the center (as shown in the photograph). Let proof in a steam oven set to 75°F (24°C), or on a rack in a turned-off oven above a bowl of boiling water, for about 1 hour.

BAKING THE BRIOCHES

Place a rack in the center of the oven and another rack directly below it. Place a heavy-duty rimmed baking sheet on the bottom rack and preheat the oven to 425°F (220°C/Gas Mark 7). Bring 1 cup (250 ml) water to a simmer. Place the brioches in the oven and carefully pour the simmering water into the rimmed sheet on the lower rack to create steam. Quickly close the oven door and bake for 18–20 minutes until golden. As soon as the brioches come out of the oven, brush them with olive oil. Transfer them to a rack and let cool.

JAM DONUTS

Beignets

Makes 6

Active time
1 hour

Bulk fermentation time
30 minutes

Freezing time
1 hour

Proofing time
30 minutes

Cooking time
3 minutes per donut

Storage
Up to 2 days in an airtight container

Equipment
- Stand mixer + dough hook
- Instant-read thermometer
- 3-in. (8-cm) round cookie cutter
- Pastry bag
- Deep fryer

Ingredients
- 2 cups (9 oz./250 g) white bread flour (T65)
- ¼ cup (2 oz./60 g) lightly beaten egg (about 1¼ eggs)
- ⅓ cup (75 g/75 ml) whole milk, well chilled
- 5 tsp (20 g) sugar
- 1.75 oz. (50 g) fresh yeast
- 1 tsp (5 g) salt
- 3 tbsp (1.75 oz./50 g) butter, diced, at room temperature
- Your choice of jam or chocolate spread (see technique p. 120) for filling
- Neutral oil for deep-frying
- Sugar for coating

PREPARING THE DOUGH

Knead the flour, egg, milk, sugar, yeast, and salt in the bowl of the stand mixer on low speed until well combined. Increase the speed to high and knead until the dough is supple and elastic. Incorporate the butter on low speed, then increase the speed and continue kneading to maintain a supple texture. Make sure the dough temperature does not exceed 77°F–79°F (25°C–26°C). Place the dough in a clean bowl and cover with plastic wrap or a clean dish towel. Let ferment for 30 minutes at room temperature. Fold the dough gently (see technique p. 48) and lay a piece of plastic wrap over the top. Flatten to a thickness of ¾ in. (2 cm) and freeze for 30 minutes. Roll the dough into a 10 × 14-in. (25 × 35-cm) rectangle, about ⅛ in. (2.5 mm) thick. Freeze for another 30 minutes.

SHAPING THE DONUTS

Using the cutter, cut out 12 × 3-in. (8-cm) disks. Place half the disks on a baking sheet lined with parchment paper. Brush a little water around the edges to moisten. Using the pastry bag, pipe jam or chocolate spread in the center of each dough disk, then cover with a second disk. Press the edges together to seal firmly. Place the donuts on a lightly floured baking sheet and let proof for about 30 minutes at room temperature in a draft-free place.

COOKING THE DONUTS

Heat the oil in the deep fryer to 340°F (170°C). Immerse the donuts in the oil, turning them over once the first side is golden to cook the other side. Drain on paper towel, then roll in sugar to coat.

LYONNAISE FRITTERS

Bugnes

Serves 6

Active time
1½ hours

Bulk fermentation time
30 minutes

Freezing time
1 hour

Proofing time
30 minutes

Cooking time
3 minutes per batch of fritters

Storage
Up to 24 hours in an airtight container

Equipment
Stand mixer + dough hook
Instant-read thermometer
Chef's knife or pasta cutter
Deep fryer

Ingredients
2 cups (9 oz./250 g) white bread flour (T65)
⅓ cup (2.75 oz./75 g) lightly beaten egg (about 1½ eggs)
¼ cup (60 g/60 ml) whole milk, well chilled
2½ tbsp (1 oz./30 g) sugar
0.25 oz. (5 g) fresh yeast
1 tsp (5 g) salt
3 tbsp (1.75 oz./50 g) butter, diced, at room temperature
2 tsp (10 g/10 ml) orange-flower water
2 tsp (10 g/10 ml) amber rum
Finely grated zest of 1 orange
Finely grated zest of 1 lemon
Neutral oil for deep-frying
Confectioners' sugar for dusting

PREPARING THE DOUGH

Knead all the ingredients, except the butter, orange-flower water, rum, and citrus zests, in the bowl of the stand mixer on low speed until well combined. Increase the speed to high and knead until the dough is supple and elastic. Incorporate the butter on low speed, then increase the speed and continue kneading to maintain a supple texture. Add the remaining ingredients and knead until just combined. Make sure the dough temperature does not exceed 77°F–79°F (25°C–26°C). Place the dough in a clean bowl and cover with plastic wrap or a clean dish towel. Let ferment for 30 minutes at room temperature. Fold the dough gently (see technique p. 48) and lay a piece of plastic wrap over the top. Flatten to a thickness of ¾ in. (2 cm) and freeze for 30 minutes. Roll the dough into a 16-in. (40-cm) square, about ⅛ in. (3.5 mm) thick. Freeze for another 30 minutes.

SHAPING THE FRITTERS

Using the chef's knife or pasta cutter, cut out strips measuring 2¾ in. (7 cm) in width, then cut the strips into diamond shapes with 1½-in. (4-cm) sides. Cut a small diagonal slit in the center of each diamond and pass a knife tip through the slits to open them up a bit. Place on a lightly floured baking sheet and let proof for about 30 minutes at room temperature in a draft-free place.

COOKING THE FRITTERS

Heat the oil in the deep fryer to 350°F (180°C). Immerse the fritters in the oil, turning them over once the first side is lightly golden. Drain on paper towel and dust with confectioners' sugar.

RING DONUTS

Makes 12

Active time

1½ hours

Bulk fermentation time

30 minutes

Freezing time

1 hour

Proofing time

30 minutes

Cooking time

3 minutes per donut

Storage time

Up to 24 hours in an airtight container

Equipment

Stand mixer + dough hook

Instant-read thermometer

3-in. (8-cm) round cookie cutter

1½-in. (4-cm) round cookie cutter

Deep fryer

Ingredients

Dough

2 cups (9 oz./250 g) white bread flour (T65)

3 tbsp (2 oz./50 g) lightly beaten egg (1 egg), well chilled

⅓ cup (90 g/90 ml) whole milk

2½ tsp (10 g) sugar

1¼ tsp (5 g) baking powder

1 tsp (5 g) salt

3 tbsp (1.75 oz./50 g) butter, diced, at room temperature

Sugar glaze

7 tbsp (3.5 oz./100 g) butter

2⅓ cups (10 oz./300 g) confectioners' sugar

5 tsp (20 g/20 ml) water

Chocolate glaze

7 oz. (200 g) dark chocolate, 70% cacao, finely chopped

Scant 1 cup (225 g/225 ml) heavy cream, min. 35% fat

2 tbsp (1 oz./30 g) butter, diced, at room temperature

To deep-fry

Neutral oil

Topping suggestions

Superfine sugar

Puffed rice cereal

Chocolate sprinkles

Hazelnut bits

PREPARING THE DOUGH

Knead all the ingredients, except the butter, in the bowl of the stand mixer on low speed until well combined. Increase the speed to high and knead until the dough is supple and elastic. Incorporate the butter on low speed, then increase the speed and knead to maintain a supple texture. Make sure the dough temperature does not exceed 77°F–79°F (25°C–26°C). Place in a clean bowl, cover with plastic wrap, and let ferment for 30 minutes at room temperature. Fold the dough gently (see technique p. 48) and lay a piece of plastic wrap over the top. Flatten to a thickness of ¾ in. (2 cm) and freeze for 30 minutes. Roll the dough into a 10 × 14-in. (25 × 35-cm) rectangle, about ⅛ in. (2.5 mm) thick. Freeze for another 30 minutes.

PREPARING THE SUGAR GLAZE

Melt the butter with the confectioners' sugar in a saucepan over low heat, stirring using a spatula. Gradually add the water, stirring after each addition until smooth. Let cool at room temperature until using.

PREPARING THE CHOCOLATE GLAZE

Place the chocolate in a heatproof bowl. Bring the cream to a boil in a saucepan and pour half of it over the chocolate. Let melt for several seconds. Pour in the remaining cream, add the butter, and stir until smooth. Let cool at room temperature, allowing it to thicken but not set.

SHAPING THE DONUTS

Cut out 12 parchment paper rectangles measuring 4 × 6 in. (10 × 15 cm) each and place on a baking sheet. Using the 3-in. (8-cm) cutter, cut out 12 dough disks, then cut out the centers using the 1½-in. (4-cm) cutter. Place each ring on a parchment rectangle near to one edge of the paper. Let proof in a steam oven set to 75°F (24°C), or place on a rack in a turned-off oven above a bowl of boiling water, for about 30 minutes.

FRYING THE DONUTS

Heat the oil in the deep fryer to 340°F (170°C). Place one donut at a time, still on the parchment paper, in the oil. The donut will slide off after a few seconds; carefully remove the paper. Once the first side is golden, turn the donut over to cook the other side. Drain on paper towel and let cool.

GLAZING AND DECORATING THE DONUTS

Dip the tops of some donuts in sugar glaze and others in chocolate glaze. Let set slightly (about 30 seconds), then sprinkle over your choice of toppings.

FRENCH TOAST WITH SUZETTE SAUCE

Pain perdu sauce Suzette

Serves 2

Active time
30 minutes

Cooking time
4 minutes per slice

Ingredients

Suzette sauce
- Scant 1/4 cup (55 g/55 ml) water
- 2/3 cup (4.5 oz./125 g) superfine sugar
- 1 cup (250 g/250 ml) orange juice
- 3 tbsp (1.5 oz./40 g) butter, diced, at room temperature
- 2 tsp (6 g) cornstarch
- 2 tbsp (30 g/30 ml) Grand Marnier

Citrus segments
- 1 orange
- 1 lime
- 1 grapefruit

French toast
- 2 eggs
- 1 cup (250 g/250 ml) whole milk
- 3 1/2 tbsp (1.5 oz./40 g) superfine sugar
- 1 tbsp finely grated orange zest (from the orange above)
- 2 slices white sourdough bread (see recipe p. 140), 3/4 in. (2 cm) thick
- 1 tbsp (15 g) butter

To serve
- Finely grated lime zest (from the lime above)
- 1 tbsp pistachio flour or confectioners' sugar (optional)

PREPARING THE SUZETTE SAUCE

Heat the water and sugar in a saucepan, stirring until the sugar dissolves. Bring to a boil and as soon as the syrup becomes a rich brown caramel, carefully pour in the orange juice, whisking to stop the cooking (watch out for splatters). Add the butter and stir until smooth. Over low heat, whisk in the cornstarch and Grand Marnier, and continue stirring until the sauce thickens. Let cool at room temperature.

PREPARING THE CITRUS SEGMENTS

Set aside 1 tbsp finely grated orange zest and the lime zest until using. Peel all the citrus fruits, taking care to remove all the white pith. Carefully cut out the segments.

PREPARING THE FRENCH TOAST

Whisk together the eggs, milk, sugar, and orange zest in a mixing bowl. Add the bread slices, pushing them down into the mixture so they are well coated on both sides. Drain well. Melt the butter in a skillet over medium heat, then add the soaked bread and cook until golden on both sides.

TO SERVE

Warm the Suzette sauce, whisking until it liquefies. While the French toast is still warm, place on serving plates and drizzle generously with the sauce. Arrange the citrus segments in an attractive pattern next to the French toast and sprinkle both with lime zest. Sprinkle with pistachio flour or dust with confectioners' sugar, if you wish. Serve immediately. Any leftover sauce can be stored in the refrigerator for a few days.

BREAD PUDDING

Serves 6

Active time

30 minutes

Infusing time

15 minutes

Cooking time

1 hour

Storage

Up to 24 hours in the refrigerator

Equipment

6 triangular pans with 3-in. (8-cm) sides, ½ in. (4 cm) deep

Ingredients

Scant 1½ cups (350 g/350 ml) whole milk

1 cup minus 3 tbsp (200 g/200 ml) heavy cream, min. 35% fat

3½ tbsp (50 g/50 ml) rum

1 tsp (3 g) ground cinnamon

3 tbsp (1.75 oz./50 g) butter, diced

1 vanilla bean, split lengthwise

7 oz. (200 g) stale bread

4 eggs

½ cup (3.5 oz./100 g) brown sugar

⅓ cup (1.75 oz./50 g) raisins

1 oz. (25 g) candied bitter orange peel, diced

Butter for the pans

Place the milk, cream, rum, cinnamon, and butter in a saucepan. Scrape in the vanilla seeds and add the bean. Bring to a boil, then remove from the heat and let infuse for 15 minutes.

Preheat the oven to 350°F (180°C/Gas Mark 4). Grease the pans with butter and place on a baking sheet.

Cut the bread into approximately ½-in. (1-cm) cubes.

Whisk the eggs and sugar together in a large bowl until thickened.

Pour the infused milk mixture into the eggs, remove the vanilla bean, and whisk to blend.

Place a layer of bread in each of the pans and scatter the raisins and candied orange peel over the top. Cover with a second layer of bread. Pour over the milk and egg mixture to cover and lightly press down using a fork.

Place the pans in a baking dish and pour in enough room-temperature water to come halfway up the sides of the pans (bain-marie). Bake for 1 hour, topping up the water in the baking dish as needed.

Carefully remove the pans from the water and place on a rack. Let the bread pudding cool to room temperature before turning it out of the pans.

SUGAR BRIOCHE TARTS

Tarte au sucre

Makes 8

Active time
1 hour

Bulk fermentation time
1 hour

Chilling time
30 minutes

Resting time
30 minutes

Proofing time
1½ hours

Cooking time
12–15 minutes

Storage
Up to 24 hours

Equipment
Stand mixer + dough hook
Instant-read thermometer

Ingredients

Brioche dough
2 cups (9 oz./250 g) all-purpose flour (*gruau*)
⅓ cup (90 g/90 ml) water
¼ cup (2 oz./60 g) lightly beaten egg (about 1¼ eggs)
1 tsp (5 g) salt
0.35 oz. (10 g) fresh yeast
4 tbsp (2.5 oz./65 g) butter, diced, at room temperature
2 tbsp (25 g) sugar

Egg wash
1 egg
1 egg yolk
2 tsp (10 g/10 ml) whole milk

Sugar crust
1 stick + 1 tsp (4 oz./120 g) butter, cut into small cubes
Scant ½ cup (2.75 oz./80 g) turbinado sugar

PREPARING THE BRIOCHE DOUGH

Knead all the dough ingredients, except the butter and sugar, in the bowl of the stand mixer on low speed for 5 minutes until well combined. Increase the speed to high and knead for 6–8 minutes until the dough is supple and elastic. With the mixer running on low speed, add the butter and sugar and knead until completely incorporated (6–8 minutes). Make sure the dough temperature does not exceed 75°F (24°C). Place in a clean bowl, cover with plastic wrap, and let ferment for 1 hour at room temperature. Fold the dough once (see technique p. 48), return it to the bowl, and cover with plastic wrap. Chill in the refrigerator for about 30 minutes.

SHAPING AND PROOFING THE BRIOCHE TARTS

Divide the dough into 8 pieces weighing 2 oz. (60 g) each. Shape into balls and let rest for 30 minutes in the refrigerator. Roll out each ball into a 4-in. (10-cm) disk and place on a baking sheet lined with parchment paper. Let proof in a steam oven set to 75°F (24°C), or place on a rack in a turned-off oven above a bowl of boiling water, for about 1½ hours.

BAKING THE BRIOCHE TARTS

Preheat the oven to 425°F (220°C/Gas Mark 7). Press down firmly on the dough disks with your fingertips to make 4 or 5 imprints on each. To make the sugar crust, whisk the egg wash ingredients together and brush over the dough disks. Place a small cube of butter in each imprint. Sprinkle turbinado sugar all over the disks and bake for 8–10 minutes until golden. Immediately transfer from the baking sheet to a rack and let cool at room temperature.

SANDWICHES AND SNACKS

FOCACCIA

Makes 4

Active time
1½ hours

Autolyse time
30 minutes

Bulk fermentation time
2 hours

Resting time
20 minutes

Proofing time
1 hour

Cooking time
15 minutes

Storage
Up to 24 hours

Equipment
Stand mixer + dough hook
Instant-read thermometer
4 × 6-in. (16-cm) baking rings, 1¾ in. (4.5 cm) deep

Ingredients

Focaccia dough
- 4 cups + 2 tbsp (1 lb. 2 oz./500 g) white bread flour (T65)
- Scant 1½ cups (330 g/330 ml) water
- 3.5 oz. (100 g) ripe liquid levain (see technique p. 40)
- 0.15 oz. (4 g) fresh yeast
- 2 tsp (10 g) salt
- Scant ½ cup (100 g/110 ml) olive oil (for *bassinage*)
- 2 tbsp (7 g) dried rosemary, finely chopped
- Olive oil for the baking rings

Toppings
- Olive oil
- Sundried tomatoes
- 2 braised artichokes, sliced
- ½ red onion, sliced
- Cheese of your choice, finely diced
- Black olives
- 1 sprig rosemary
- Salt

PREPARING THE DOUGH
Knead the flour and water in the bowl of the stand mixer on low speed for 5 minutes until no dry bits remain. Cover the bowl with plastic wrap and let rest for 30 minutes at room temperature (autolyse). Add the levain, yeast, and salt and knead on high speed for 5 minutes until the dough is well blended and supple (it should wrap around the dough hook). With the mixer running on low speed, gradually add the scant ½ cup (100 g/110 ml) olive oil, as needed, depending on the consistency of the dough, which should be soft and supple (*bassinage*). Knead until the oil is absorbed, then knead in the rosemary. Make sure the dough temperature does not exceed 73°F–75°F (23°C–24°C). Transfer the dough to a clean bowl lightly greased with olive oil and cover with a dish towel. Let the dough ferment for 30 minutes at room temperature and then give it one fold (see technique p. 48). Cover with plastic wrap and let ferment for another 30 minutes, then perform a second and final fold. Let the dough ferment undisturbed for an additional 1 hour at room temperature.

SHAPING AND PROOFING THE DOUGH
Place the baking rings on a baking sheet lined with parchment paper, then line the insides of the rings with parchment paper, too. Brush the insides and the rims of the rings with olive oil. Divide the dough into 4 pieces weighing 9 oz. (250 g) each. Shape them into very loose balls and place inside the rings. Cover with plastic wrap and let rest for 20 minutes at room temperature. Using your fingertips, gently stretch the dough to fill the circles. Let proof for 1 hour at room temperature in a draft-free place.

TOPPING AND BAKING THE FOCACCIAS
Place a rack in the center of the oven and another rack directly below it. Place a heavy-duty rimmed baking sheet on the bottom rack and preheat the oven to 515°F (270°C/Gas Mark 10). Bring 1 cup (250 ml) water to a simmer. Liberally drizzle the focaccia dough with olive oil to cover. Using your fingertips, make deep craters all over the surface of each focaccia and sprinkle with salt. Arrange sun-dried tomatoes and artichoke and onion slices over the focaccias, then add the cheese, a few olives, and some rosemary leaves. Place the baking sheet with the rings on the rack in the center of the oven and carefully pour the simmering water into the rimmed sheet on the lower rack to create steam. Quickly close the oven door and bake for 15 minutes. Remove from the oven as soon as the parts of dough that have bubbled up begin to brown.

ALSATIAN PIZZA

Flammekueche

Makes 3 pizzas to serve 6

Active time

1 hour

Bulk fermentation time

1 hour + overnight

Resting time

15 minutes

Proofing time

30 minutes

Cooking time

10–15 minutes per pizza + 15 minutes for frying onions

Storage

Up to 24 hours

Equipment

Stand mixer + dough hook

Instant-read thermometer

Ingredients

Alsatian pizza dough

4 cups + 2 tbsp (1 lb. 2 oz./500 g) white bread flour (T65)

1⅓ cups (320 g/320 ml) water

1¾ tsp (9 g) salt

0.25 oz. (5 g) fresh yeast

4½ tsp (20 g/22 ml) olive oil

Toppings

2 large onions

Olive oil

Scant 1 cup (7 oz./200 g) crème fraîche

⅔ cup (5.25 oz./150 g) *fromage blanc* (or substitute strained greek yogurt, quark, or ricotta)

1 pinch freshly grated nutmeg

5.25 oz. (150 g) smoked bacon, thinly sliced crosswise (*lardons*)

Salt and freshly ground pepper

PREPARING THE ALSATIAN PIZZA DOUGH (1 DAY AHEAD)

Knead all the dough ingredients in the bowl of the stand mixer on low speed for 5 minutes until well combined. Increase the speed to high and knead for 5 minutes until the dough is supple and elastic. Make sure the dough temperature does not exceed 75°F (24°C). Place in a clean bowl, cover with plastic wrap, and let ferment for 1 hour at room temperature. Fold the dough once (see technique p. 48), place it back in the bowl, and cover with plastic wrap. Let ferment overnight in the refrigerator.

SHAPING AND PROOFING THE DOUGH

The next day, divide the dough into 3 equal pieces and gently shape each one into a ball. Let rest for 15 minutes at room temperature. Roll each piece of dough into an approximate 8 × 12-in. (20 × 30-cm) oval and place on baking sheets lined with parchment paper. Let proof in a steam oven set to 75°F (24°C), or on racks in a turned-off oven above a bowl of boiling water, for 30 minutes.

PREPARING THE TOPPINGS

Slice the onions very thinly and cook them in a skillet with a little olive oil over low heat until softened and translucent. Meanwhile, stir together the crème fraîche and *fromage blanc* in a bowl until well combined. Season with nutmeg, salt, and pepper.

BAKING THE ALSATIAN PIZZA

Preheat the oven to 515°F (270°C/Gas Mark 10). Spread the cream mixture evenly over the ovals of dough and scatter with the onions and bacon. Bake each pizza for 10–15 minutes, until the cream mixture just begins to brown and the crust is lightly golden. Serve immediately.

HAM AND TOMATO PIZZA

Pizza jambon tomate

Makes 3 × 10–12-in. (25–30-cm) pizzas

Active time
1 hour

Bulk fermentation time
1 hour + overnight in the refrigerator

Resting time
15 minutes

Proofing time
30 minutes

Cooking time
8–10 minutes per pizza

Storage
Up to 24 hours

Equipment
- Stand mixer + dough hook
- Instant-read thermometer
- Heavy-duty baking sheet or baking stone

Ingredients

Pizza dough
- 4 cups + 2 tbsp (1 lb. 2 oz./500 g) white bread flour (T65)
- 1⅓ cups (320 g/320 ml) water
- 1¾ tsp (9 g) salt
- 0.25 oz. (5 g) fresh yeast
- 4½ tsp (20 g/22 ml) olive oil

Toppings
- 2½ cups (1 lb. 5 oz./600 g) tomato sauce
- 3 balls mozzarella
- Button mushrooms
- Cherry tomatoes
- 12 slices prosciutto or another cured ham
- Arugula and basil leaves

PREPARING THE DOUGH (1 DAY AHEAD)

Knead all the pizza dough ingredients in the bowl of the stand mixer on low speed for 5 minutes until well combined. Increase the speed to medium and knead for 5 minutes until the dough is supple. Make sure the dough temperature does not exceed 75°F (24°C). Cover the bowl with plastic wrap and let ferment for 1 hour at room temperature. Fold the dough once (see technique p. 48) and shape it into a ball. Place in a clean bowl, cover with plastic wrap, and let ferment overnight in the refrigerator.

SHAPING AND PROOFING THE DOUGH

The next day, divide the dough into 3 pieces weighing 10 oz. (280 g) each. Shape into balls, cover with plastic wrap, and let rest for 15 minutes at room temperature. Roll out or stretch each piece of dough into a 10–12-in. (25–30-cm) disk and place on baking sheets lined with parchment paper. Let proof in a steam oven set to 75°F (24°C), or on a rack in a turned-off oven above a bowl of boiling water, for 30 minutes.

TOPPING THE PIZZAS

Divide the tomato sauce between the pizzas and spread into a thin, even layer. Cut the mozzarella and mushrooms into thin slices and scatter evenly over the sauce. Cut the cherry tomatoes in half and arrange over the mush-rooms and mozzarella.

BAKING THE PIZZAS

Place a heavy-duty baking sheet or baking stone on a rack in the center of the oven and preheat the oven to 515°F (270°C/Gas Mark 10). Slide one of the pizzas, still on the parchment paper, onto the hot baking sheet or baking stone in the oven and bake for 8–10 minutes. Repeat with the remaining pizzas, baking them one at a time. As soon as they come out of the oven, scatter over the ham slices and arugula and basil leaves. Serve immediately.

PASTRAMI BAGELS

Bagel au pastrami

Makes 8

Active time

1½ hours

Bulk fermentation time

15 minutes

Resting time

15 minutes

Proofing time

45 minutes

Cooking time

15–20 minutes
+ poaching the bagels

Storage

Filled bagels: up to 24 hours

Unfilled bagels: several days well covered in plastic wrap

Equipment

Stand mixer + dough hook

Instant-read thermometer

Ingredients

Bagel dough

4 cups + 2 tbsp (1 lb. 2 oz./500 g) all-purpose flour (T55)

1 cup minus 3 tbsp (200 g/200 ml) whole milk

Scant ½ cup (100 g/100 ml) water

1¾ tsp (9 g) salt

3 tbsp (1.5 oz./40 g) butter, diced, at room temperature

0.25 oz. (5 g) fresh yeast

2 tsp (10 g) honey of your choice

3.5 oz. (100 g) ripe stiff levain (see technique p. 38)

Egg wash

1 egg white

Toppings

Sesame or poppy seeds

Fillings

1 cucumber

Lettuce leaves of your choice

2 large red onions

Cornichons

1 cup (9 oz./250 g) cream cheese

2 tsp (10 g) Dijon mustard

16 slices pastrami

PREPARING THE DOUGH

Knead all the bagel dough ingredients in the bowl of the stand mixer on low speed for 3 minutes until well combined. Increase the speed to high and knead for 8 minutes until the dough is supple and elastic. Make sure the dough temperature does not exceed 75°F (24°C). Place in a clean bowl, cover with plastic wrap, and let ferment for 15 minutes at room temperature. Divide the dough into 8 pieces weighing 4.25 oz. (120 g) each and gently shape each one into a ball. Let rest for 15 minutes at room temperature.

SHAPING AND PROOFING THE DOUGH

Shape each piece of dough into a log measuring 6 in. (15 cm) in length. Join the ends of each log together to make 8 rings and place on a baking sheet lined with parchment paper. Let proof in a steam oven set to 75°F (24°C), or on a rack in a turned-off oven above a bowl of boiling water, for 45 minutes.

COOKING THE BAGELS

Preheat the oven to 425°F (220°C/Gas Mark 7) and bring a large saucepan of water to a boil. Poach the bagels in the boiling water for about 30 seconds on each side. Drain with a slotted spoon and return to the parchment-lined baking sheet. Lightly whisk the egg white and brush over the bagels. Sprinkle with sesame or poppy seeds and bake for 15–20 minutes. Let cool completely on a rack before slicing and filling.

FILLING THE BAGELS

Wash the cucumber and lettuce and slice them thinly. Peel and thinly slice the red onions and cut the cornichons in half lengthwise. Mash the cream cheese with a fork to make it easier to spread, then mix in the mustard until well blended. Cut the bagels in half horizontally and generously spread the cut sides with the mustard cream cheese. Scatter the red onion and lettuce over the bottom halves and top with the pastrami, cucumber, and cornichons. Place the tops on the bagels and serve immediately.

CHEFS' NOTES

To make black bagels, add 1 oz. (25 g) activated charcoal powder (*charbon végétal*) to the bagel dough.

SALMON POLARBRØD

Pain polaire au saumon

Makes 16 small sandwiches (12 polarbrød)

Active time

1½ hours

Bulk fermentation time

1 hour

Resting time

30 minutes in the refrigerator

Cooking time

2 minutes per polarbrød

Storage

Filled polarbrød: up to 24 hours

Unfilled polarbrød: several days in the refrigerator in an airtight container, or well covered in plastic wrap

Equipment

Stand mixer + dough hook

Dough docker or fork

Skillet

Ingredients

Dough

2¾ cups (12.5 oz./350 g) white bread flour (T65)

Scant 1½ cups (5.25 oz./150 g) rye flour

1 cup (250 g/250 ml) water at 39°F (4°C)

2.5 oz. (75 g) ripe liquid levain (see technique p. 40)

⅓ cup (75 g/75 ml) heavy cream, min. 35% fat

2½ tbsp (2 oz./50 g) glucose syrup

0.35 oz. (10 g) fresh yeast

1¼ tsp (5 g) baking powder

Scant ½ tsp (1 g) ground fennel (optional)

Scant 2½ tsp (12 g) salt

Oil for cooking

Fillings

1 lemon

1 cucumber

½ bunch dill

1 cup (9 oz./250 g) cream cheese

A few pink peppercorns

8 slices smoked salmon

A few leaves purslane

PREPARING THE DOUGH

Knead all the ingredients, except the oil for cooking, in the bowl of the stand mixer on low speed for 5 minutes until well combined. Increase the speed to high and knead for 4 minutes until the dough is smooth. Shape into a ball, cover with plastic wrap, and let ferment for 1 hour at room temperature.

SHAPING THE DOUGH

Divide the dough into 12 pieces weighing 2.75–3.25 oz. (80–90 g) each and shape into balls. Cover with plastic wrap and let rest for at least 30 minutes in the refrigerator. Roll each piece into a 6–7-in. (15–18-cm) disk. Pierce each disk all over with the dough docker or a fork.

COOKING THE POLARBRØD

Grease the skillet with a little oil using a paper towel. Warm the skillet over medium heat and cook each polarbrød for about 1 minute on each side until just starting to brown. Transfer to a baking sheet lined with parchment paper to cool. Store the polarbrød in an airtight container or covered in plastic wrap to keep them soft.

FILLING THE POLARBRØD

Cut the lemon in half crosswise; juice one of the halves and cut the other half into quarters. Peel strips from the cucumber if you wish, then thinly slice it crosswise. Roughly chop the dill. Stir together the cream cheese, lemon juice, dill, and pink peppercorns in a bowl until well blended. Gently reheat the polarbrød in the oven or a toaster. Generously spread the tops of 4 polarbrød with the cream cheese mixture, then add cucumber slices and 1 slice of salmon to each one. Cover with a second polarbrød and press down gently with your hand. Spread with another layer of the cream cheese mixture and top with cucumber slices and a second slice of salmon. Cover with the remaining polarbrød, press down gently, and cut into quarters using a serrated knife.

FALAFEL-FILLED PITA BREADS

Pita aux falafels

Makes 10

Active time
1½ hours

Bulk fermentation time
1 hour

Resting time
30 minutes

Cooking time
2 minutes per batch

Storage
Unfilled pita breads: up to 2 days in the refrigerator covered in plastic wrap, or freeze

Equipment
Stand mixer + dough hook
Instant-read thermometer
Heavy-duty baking sheet or baking stone

Ingredients

Pita bread dough
4 cups + 2 tbsp (1 lb. 2 oz./500 g) white bread flour (T65)
1¼ cups (300 g/300 ml) water
7 oz. (200 g) ripe liquid levain (see technique p. 40)
1¾ tsp (9 g) salt

To shape
Fine semolina flour

Fillings
5 tomatoes
1 cucumber
2 large red onions
30 falafels (homemade or store-bought)
1 lb. (500 g) hummus (homemade or store-bought)
1 bunch cilantro

PREPARING THE DOUGH

Knead all the pita bread dough ingredients in the bowl of the stand mixer on low speed for 3 minutes until well combined. Increase the speed to medium and knead for 5 minutes until the dough is supple. Make sure the dough temperature does not exceed 73°F–75°F (23°C–24°C). Cover the bowl with plastic wrap and let ferment for 1 hour at room temperature. Divide the dough into 10 pieces weighing 3.5 oz. (100 g) each. Shape the pieces into balls, dust with semolina flour, and cover with a clean dish towel. Let rest for 30 minutes at room temperature.

SHAPING THE DOUGH

Place a heavy-duty baking sheet or baking stone on a rack in the center of the oven and preheat the oven to 515°F (270°C/Gas Mark 10). Generously flour a work surface and rolling pin with semolina flour to prevent the dough from sticking and tearing. Roll each piece of dough into very thin 8-in. (20-cm) disks and place on parchment paper.

BAKING THE PITA BREADS

Slide the parchment paper with the pitas on it onto the hot baking sheet or baking stone in the oven and bake for about 2 minutes, baking in batches if necessary. A few small bubbles will form in the dough, which will grow and join together to make the pita puff up like a balloon. Remove the pitas from the oven as soon as they are completely puffed but still pale. Take care not to overbake them, as they will no longer be pliable. Alternatively, you can cook the pitas in a very hot ungreased skillet. To do this, cook one pita at a time for 30 seconds on one side, then turn it over and cook for 1–2 minutes until it has puffed (the pitas will not puff as reliably as if you bake them in the oven). Turn the pita over and cook for about 1 minute until pale golden on the other side. Stack the pitas on top of one another and cover with a damp dish towel to keep them soft and moist.

FILLING THE PITA BREADS

Slice the tomatoes and cucumber crosswise and thinly slice the red onions. Warm the falafels in a skillet over low heat. Warm the pita breads under the broiler for a few minutes then cut them open along one side. Open the pitas and spread the insides generously with hummus, then fill with the cucumber, tomatoes, onion, falafels, and a few cilantro leaves. Serve immediately.

TOMATO, MOZZARELLA, AND PESTO PANINI

Panini tomate, mozzarella et pesto

Makes 8

Active time

1½ hours

Bulk fermentation time

1 hour + overnight

Resting time

15 minutes

Proofing time

1 hour

Cooking time

About 20 minutes

Storage

Ungrilled filled panini: up to 24 hours

Unfilled panini: up to 2 days well covered in plastic wrap

Equipment

Stand mixer + dough hook

Instant-read thermometer

Grill pan (optional)

Ingredients

Panini roll dough

4 cups + 2 tbsp (1 lb. 2 oz./500 g) white bread flour (T65)

1⅓ cups (320 g/320 ml) water

1¾ tsp (9 g) salt

0.25 oz. (5 g) fresh yeast

4½ tsp (20 g/22 ml) olive oil

Fillings

8 cocktail tomatoes

4 mozzarella balls (4.5 oz./125 g each)

½ cup (3.5 oz./100 g) basil or arugula pesto

Arugula

PREPARING THE DOUGH (1 DAY AHEAD)

Knead all the dough ingredients in the bowl of the stand mixer on low speed for 5 minutes until well combined. Increase the speed to medium and knead for 5 minutes until the dough is supple. Make sure the dough temperature does not exceed 75°F (24°C). Cover the bowl with plastic wrap and let ferment for 1 hour at room temperature. Fold the dough (see technique p. 48), place in a clean bowl, and cover with plastic wrap. Let ferment overnight in the refrigerator.

SHAPING AND PROOFING THE DOUGH

The next day, divide the dough into 8 pieces weighing 3.75 oz. (105 g) each and shape into balls. Let rest for 15 minutes at room temperature. Shape each piece of dough into a mini baguette measuring 7 in. (18 cm) in length (see technique p. 51) and place on a baking sheet lined with parchment paper. Let proof in a steam oven set to 75°F (24°C), or on a rack in a turned-off oven above a bowl of boiling water, for 1 hour.

BAKING THE PANINI ROLLS

Place a rack in the center of the oven and another rack directly below it. Place a heavy-duty rimmed baking sheet on the bottom rack and preheat the oven to 450°F (240°C/Gas Mark 8). Bring 1 cup (250 ml) water to a simmer. Place the rolls in the oven and carefully pour the simmering water into the rimmed sheet on the lower rack to create steam. Quickly close the oven door and bake for 6–8 minutes until just cooked through but not browned. The rolls should remain white, so keep a close eye on them. Immediately transfer the rolls to a rack and let them cool completely at room temperature.

FILLING THE PANINI ROLLS

Wash and slice the tomatoes crosswise, then evenly slice the mozzarella. Cut the panini rolls in half horizontally and spread the cut sides of each with about 1 tbsp pesto. Top the bottom halves with tomato and mozzarella slices. Place the tops on the panini rolls and cook on a grill pan for about 10 minutes (5 minutes on each side), until the mozzarella melts and the rolls are golden. Alternatively, place the panini under the broiler in the oven set to 480°F (250°C/Gas Mark 9). Serve immediately.

VEGETARIAN BLACK BUN BURGERS

Black burger végétarien

Makes 8

Active time

1½ hours

***Pâte fermentée* fermentation time**

Overnight

Bulk fermentation time

45 minutes

Resting time

15 minutes

Proofing time

1¼–1½ hours

Cooking time

20–25 minutes + frying the burgers

Storage

Unfilled buns: up to several days well covered in plastic wrap

Equipment

Stand mixer + dough hook

Instant-read thermometer

8 × 4-in. (10-cm) cake rings, 1¼ in. (3 cm) deep

Ingredients

Pâte fermentée

½ cup (2.5 oz./70 g) white bread flour (T65)

3 tbsp (43 g/43 ml) water

Scant ¼ tsp (1 g) salt

0.05 oz. (1 g) fresh yeast

Black bun dough

4 cups + 2 tbsp (1 lb. 2 oz./500 g) white bread flour (T65)

1 oz. (25 g) activated charcoal powder (*charbon végétal*)

1 cup (250 g/250 ml) water

2 tsp (10 g) salt

5 tsp (25 g) milk powder

1 oz. (25 g) fresh yeast

2 tbsp (25 g) superfine sugar

4 oz. (115 g) *pâte fermentée* (see left)

3 tbsp (1.75 oz./50 g) butter, diced, at room temperature

Egg wash

1 egg

1 egg yolk

2 tsp (10 g/10 ml) whole milk

Topping

Sesame seeds

Fillings

1 cucumber

Lettuce leaves of your choice

4 scallions

2 large red onions

2 cups (1 lb. 2 oz./500 g) greek-style yogurt

2 tbsp (27 g/30 ml) sesame oil

Vegetable oil

8 vegetarian patties of your choice

9 oz. (250 g) cherry tomatoes, slow-roasted

Salt and freshly ground pepper

CHEFS' NOTES

To make classic hamburger buns, simply omit the charcoal powder.

PREPARING THE PÂTE FERMENTÉE (1 DAY AHEAD)

Mix the flour, water, salt, and yeast together in the bowl of the stand mixer and knead on low speed, or by hand, for 10 minutes until smooth. Place in a bowl, cover in plastic wrap, and let ferment overnight in the refrigerator.

PREPARING THE DOUGH

Knead all the black bun dough ingredients in the bowl of the stand mixer on low speed for 3 minutes until well combined. Increase the speed to high and knead for 7 minutes until the dough is supple and elastic. Make sure the dough temperature does not exceed 75°F (24°C). Cover with plastic wrap and let ferment for 45 minutes at room temperature. Divide the dough into 8 pieces weighing about 4.5 oz. (125 g) each, and gently shape each one into a ball. Let rest for 15 minutes at room temperature.

SHAPING AND PROOFING THE DOUGH

Place the cake rings on a baking sheet lined with parchment paper. Shape the pieces of dough into tight balls and place in the rings. Let proof in a steam oven set to 75°F (24°C), or on a rack in a turned-off oven above a bowl of boiling water, for 1¼–1½ hours.

BAKING THE BLACK BUNS

Place a rack in the center of the oven and another rack directly below it. Place a heavy-duty rimmed baking sheet on the bottom rack and preheat the oven to 425°F (220°C/Gas Mark 7). Bring 1 cup (250 ml) water to a simmer. Whisk the egg wash ingredients together and brush over the buns. Sprinkle them with sesame seeds and place in the oven. Carefully pour the simmering water into the rimmed sheet on the lower rack to create steam. Quickly close the oven door and bake the buns for 20–25 minutes. Immediately remove the buns from the rings and let them cool completely on a rack.

FILLING THE BURGER BUNS

Wash the cucumber, lettuce, and scallions. Slice the cucumber. Thinly slice the red onions and scallions. Whisk together the scallions, yogurt, and sesame oil in a bowl and season with salt and pepper. Preheat the broiler. Cut the buns in half horizontally and place under the broiler briefly to toast. Warm a little vegetable oil in a skillet over medium heat. Add the vegetarian patties and cook on both sides until browned. Spread the insides of the buns with yogurt sauce and arrange lettuce, cherry tomatoes, red onion, and cucumber over the bottom halves. Add the vegetarian patties, spread over a little sauce, and finish with another piece of lettuce. Place the tops on the burgers and serve immediately.

CHICKEN BAO BUNS

Gua bao au poulet

Makes 10

Active time
1 hour

Bulk fermentation time
30 minutes

Proofing time
10 minutes

Marinating time
30 minutes

Cooking time
13 minutes

Storage
Unfilled buns: up to several days wrapped in a clean dish towel

Equipment
- Instant-read thermometer
- Stand mixer + dough hook
- 3-in. (8-cm) round cookie cutter
- Bamboo steamer

Ingredients

Bao buns
- Scant 1 cup (225 g/225 ml) low-fat milk
- 1½ cups (6.5 oz./185 g) all-purpose flour (T55)
- 1½ cups (6.5 oz./185 g) pastry flour (T45)
- 0.25 oz. (5 g) fresh yeast
- 1 tsp (4 g) baking powder
- 3 tbsp (1¼ oz./35 g) sugar
- ⅓ cup (75 g/80 ml) grape-seed oil

Fillings
- 5 tbsp soy sauce
- 2½ tsp (12 g) honey
- 2–3 cloves garlic
- 2–3 chicken breasts
- 1 cucumber
- 1 lb. (500 g) shredded white cabbage and julienned carrot salad
- 5 leaves lettuce
- Several sprigs cilantro

PREPARING THE DOUGH

Warm the milk to 91°F (33°C). Knead the all-purpose and pastry flours, yeast, baking powder, sugar, and oil in the bowl of the stand mixer on low speed until well combined. Pour in the milk and knead on high speed until incorporated. Shape the dough into a ball, place in a clean bowl, and cover the bowl loosely with plastic wrap. Let ferment for 30 minutes at room temperature, or until doubled in volume.

SHAPING AND PROOFING THE DOUGH

Roll the dough to a thickness of about ¼ in. (5 mm). Cut out 10 disks using the 3-in. (8-cm) cookie cutter, brush them with grape-seed oil, and fold them in two to make half-circles. Place on a baking sheet lined with parchment paper and let proof in a steam oven set to 95°F (35°C), or on a rack in a turned-off oven above a bowl of boiling water, for about 10 minutes.

COOKING THE BAO BUNS

Pour about 1½ in. (4 cm) water into a large skillet or pot and bring to a boil. Place the buns in the steamer and carefully lower it into the skillet. Cook covered for 3 minutes over low-medium heat. Open to release steam, then replace the lid and cook for an additional 2 minutes. Open again, replace the lid, and cook for an additional 8 minutes until puffed and cooked through.

FILLING THE BAO BUNS

Combine the soy sauce, honey, and garlic in a bowl and whisk to blend. Marinate the chicken in this mixture for about 30 minutes. Drain the chicken well and cook it in a skillet over low heat on both sides until cooked through and browned. Warm the bao buns briefly under the broiler. Cut the chicken into bite-sized pieces and drizzle with the pan juices, then peel the cucumber and cut it into half-moon slices. Preheat the oven to 350°F (180°C/Gas Mark 4). Fill the buns with chicken, cabbage and carrot salad, cucumber, lettuce, and cilantro leaves. Place on a baking sheet lined with parchment paper and warm in the oven for 5 minutes. Serve warm.

PAN BAGNAT

Makes 8

Active time

1½ hours

Milk levain fermentation time

3 hours

Bulk fermentation time

1½ hours

Resting time

30 minutes + 2 hours before serving

Proofing time

1 hour

Cooking time

16 minutes

Storage

Unfilled rolls: up to several days wrapped in a clean dish towel

Equipment

Stand mixer + dough hook

Oven thermometer

Instant-read thermometer

Baker's couche (optional)

Heavy-duty baking sheet or baking stone

Bread lame

Ingredients

Milk levain

2 tbsp (30 g/30 ml) whole milk at 113°F (45°C)

¾ cup + 2 tbsp (3.5 oz./100 g) white bread flour (T65)

5.25 oz. (150 g) ripe liquid levain (see technique p. 40)

Pan bagnat rolls

10 oz. (280 g) milk levain (see above)

2 cups (9 oz./250 g) white bread flour (T65)

2¼ cups (9 oz./250 g) white whole wheat flour (T80)

1½ cups (375 g/375 ml) water

Scant 2½ tsp (12 g) salt

¼ cup (50 g/56 ml) olive oil (for *bassinage*)

Fillings

8 small tomatoes

8 hard-boiled eggs

2 large red onions

2 green chili peppers

2 cloves garlic

½ cup (100 g/112 ml) extra virgin olive oil

8 leaves lettuce

40 pitted black olives

14 oz. (400 g) canned tuna fillets packed in water, drained

24 anchovy fillets packed in olive oil, drained

Basil leaves

PREPARING THE MILK LEVAIN (1 DAY AHEAD)
Knead all the milk levain ingredients in the bowl of the stand mixer on low speed for 5 minutes until well combined. Shape into a very tight ball and cut a cross on the top. Place in a clean bowl and cover with a clean dish towel. Let ferment for 3 hours at 95°F (35°C), or in an oven preheated to 86°F–104°F (30°C–40°C; use an oven thermometer to check the temperature) and then turned off, until cracks form on the surface.

PREPARING THE DOUGH (1 DAY AHEAD)
Knead all the pan bagnat dough ingredients, except the olive oil, in the bowl of the stand mixer on low speed for 5 minutes until well combined. Increase the speed to high and knead for 6 minutes until the dough is supple, smooth, and elastic. Drizzle in the olive oil in 3 equal quantities, kneading the dough after each addition until it is supple and smooth (*bassinage*). Make sure the dough temperature does not exceed 75°F–77°F (24°C–25°C). Place the dough in a clean bowl, cover with plastic wrap, and let ferment for 1½ hours at room temperature. Divide the dough into 8 pieces weighing 5.25 oz. (150 g) each and shape into loose balls. Cover with plastic wrap and let rest for 30 minutes at room temperature.

SHAPING AND PROOFING THE DOUGH (1 DAY AHEAD)
Flatten each piece of dough into a thick 6-in. (16-cm) disk and place on a floured baker's couche or clean, heavy dish towel with the seam facing up. Pleat the couche or towel around the dough pieces like an accordion and let proof for 1 hour at room temperature in a draft-free place.

SCORING AND BAKING THE ROLLS (1 DAY AHEAD)
Place a heavy-duty baking sheet or baking stone on a rack in the center of the oven and a heavy-duty rimmed baking sheet on the bottom rack. Preheat the oven to 480°F (250°C/Gas Mark 10) and bring 1 cup (250 ml) water to a simmer. Invert the pieces of dough onto a piece of parchment paper and score a large cross-shaped cut into the top of each one using the bread lame. Slide the parchment paper onto the hot baking sheet or baking stone in the center and carefully pour the simmering water into the rimmed sheet on the lower rack to create steam. Quickly close the oven door and bake for about 16 minutes until pale golden. Take care not to overbake the rolls, as they will be dry. Immediately transfer the rolls to a rack and let them cool completely at room temperature, before storing.

ASSEMBLING THE PAN BAGNAT
The next day, cut the rolls in half horizontally. Slice the tomatoes and eggs crosswise and thinly slice the onions and chili peppers. Crush the garlic into a bowl, add the olive oil, and stir to blend. Season with salt and pepper and divide between the roll bases. Arrange the lettuce leaves, tomatoes, eggs, onions, chili peppers, olives, tuna, and anchovies over the bases and garnish with a few basil leaves. Place the tops on the rolls and let rest for 2 hours before serving.

CHEFS' NOTES

• Milk levain provides the same strength as a classic stiff levain and has a similar fermentation process, but the aroma and flavor are much milder, with minimal acidity. If you prefer more distinctive sourdough notes, use 10 oz. (280 g) ripe stiff levain in the dough instead (see technique p. 38).

• Letting the bread dry out for a day before filling it prevents it from turning soggy when filled.

CHEESE AND VEGETABLE WRAPS

Wrap au fromage et légumes

Makes 20

Active time

1 hour

Resting time

30 minutes in the refrigerator

Cooking time

40 seconds–1 minute per flatbread

Storage

Filled wraps: up to 24 hours

Unfilled flatbreads: several days in an airtight container or well covered in plastic wrap

Equipment

Stand mixer + dough hook

Skillet

Ingredients

Dough

4 cups + 2 tbsp (1 lb. 2 oz./500 g) white bread flour (T65), plus extra for coating

⅓ cup (1.75 oz./50 g) semolina flour (medium grind)

1⅓ cups (320 g/320 ml) cold water

⅓ cup (75 g/80 ml) grape-seed oil, plus extra for greasing

1¾ tsp (9 g) salt

For rolling

Bread flour and semolina flour, as needed

Fillings

8 carrots

4 tbsp sesame oil

4 tsp cider vinegar

1 container sprouts of your choice, divided

10 dill or Russian-style malossol pickles

20 slices cheese (such as Comté)

Salt and freshly ground pepper

PREPARING THE DOUGH

Knead all the ingredients in the bowl of the stand mixer on low speed until well combined and smooth. Shape the dough into 20 balls weighing 1.5 oz. (45 g) each. Coat with flour, cover with plastic wrap, and let rest for at least 30 minutes in the refrigerator.

SHAPING THE DOUGH

Using plenty of bread flour and semolina flour to prevent sticking, roll each piece of dough into a very thin disk, 8–10 in. (20–25 cm) in diameter.

COOKING THE FLATBREADS

Using a paper towel, grease the skillet with a thin layer of oil. Warm the skillet over high heat until it is very hot. Cook each flatbread for about 20 seconds on each side, turning them over and removing them from the skillet at the first sign of browning. As soon as the flatbreads have cooked, stack them on top of one another and cover with a damp dish towel to keep them moist.

FILLING THE FLATBREADS

Peel and grate the carrots on the large holes of a box grater. Place in a bowl with the sesame oil, vinegar, and half the sprouts. Season with salt and pepper and stir to blend. Cut the pickles lengthwise into thin slices. Reheat the flatbreads for a few minutes in a warm oven. Top each one with 1 slice of cheese, pickle slices, and the grated carrot mixture. Roll up the flatbreads and cut them in two. Wrap a strip of parchment paper around each half at the base and tie with string to hold in place. Sprinkle the remaining sprouts over the tops and serve.

REVISITED PARISIAN HAM SANDWICH

Parisien revisité

Makes 8

Active time
2 hours

Bulk fermentation time
30 minutes

Resting time
1–1½ hours

Proofing time
1½ hours

Cooking time
22–24 minutes

Storage
Filled sandwiches: up to 24 hours

Unfilled rolls: up to several days wrapped in a clean dish towel

Equipment
Stand mixer + dough hook

Instant-read thermometer

Bread lame

Serrated knife

Ingredients

Yeasted puff pastry rolls

Base dough

4 cups + 2 tbsp (1 lb. 2 oz./500 g) strong white bread flour (T65)

1 cup + 5 tsp (270 g/270 ml) water

0.25 oz. (5 g) fresh yeast

3.5 oz. (100 g) ripe stiff levain (see technique p. 38)

1¾ tsp (9 g) salt

Laminating butter

1¾ sticks (7 oz./200 g) butter, preferably 84% fat

Mustard butter

1¾ sticks (7 oz./200 g) butter, softened

¼ cup (1.75 oz./50 g) whole grain mustard

Fillings

8 slices ham (*jambon blanc*)

Several cornichons, thinly sliced (optional)

PREPARING THE YEASTED PUFF PASTRY DOUGH

Knead all the base dough ingredients in the bowl of the stand mixer on low speed until well combined. Increase the speed to high and knead for 5 minutes until the dough is supple and elastic. The dough temperature should be about 75°F (24°C). Roll the dough into a 6 × 12-in. (15 × 30-cm) rectangle, cover with plastic wrap, and let ferment for 30 minutes in the refrigerator. Roll the 84% butter into a 6-in. (15-cm) square (see technique p. 62). Place the butter in the center of the dough and fold the dough over it to enclose the butter completely. Roll the dough into an approximate 8 × 20-in. (20 × 50-cm) rectangle, then fold the shorter ends of the dough inward, one-third of the way down from the top and two-thirds of the way up from the bottom. Fold the dough in half, like a book, to make a double turn (see technique p. 65). Let rest for 15–30 minutes in the refrigerator. Give the dough a quarter turn clockwise, so that the flap is on one side, and roll it into an approximate 8 × 20-in. (20 × 50-cm) rectangle. Fold the bottom third of the dough upward, then fold the top third down over the top to make a single turn (see technique p. 64). Let rest for 30 minutes in the refrigerator.

SHAPING AND PROOFING THE DOUGH

Divide the dough into 8 equal pieces. Shape into balls, cover with plastic wrap, and let rest for 15–30 minutes in the refrigerator. Shape into small baguettes measuring 8 in. (20 cm) in length (see technique p. 51), and place on a baking sheet lined with parchment paper. Using the bread lame, score each loaf lengthwise down the center. Let proof in a steam oven set to 75°F (24°C), or on a rack in a turned-off oven above a bowl of boiling water, for 1½ hours.

BAKING THE ROLLS

Preheat the oven to 400°F (200°C/Gas Mark 6). Bake for 22–24 minutes. Let cool completely on a rack.

PREPARING THE MUSTARD BUTTER

Place the butter and mustard in a bowl and mix until well blended.

PREPARING THE SANDWICHES

Using the serrated knife, cut the rolls in half horizontally and spread the cut sides with the mustard butter. Place a slice of ham on each bottom half, along with a few cornichon slices, if you wish. Place the tops on the sandwiches and serve.

REVISITED CROQUE-MONSIEUR

Croque-monsieur revisité

Makes 6

Active time
30 minutes

Cooking time
15–20 minutes

Storage
Up to 24 hours

Ingredients

Mustard butter

- 1½ sticks (6 oz./180 g) butter, softened
- 4 tsp (20 g) whole grain mustard

Emmentaler spread

- 3½ cups (14 oz./400 g) grated Emmentaler cheese
- Scant 1 cup (200 g/200 ml) heavy cream, min. 35% fat

Croque-monsieurs

- 6 slices white sourdough bread (see recipe p. 140)
- 6 slices ham (*jambon blanc*)

PREPARING THE MUSTARD BUTTER

Place the butter and mustard in a bowl and stir until well blended.

PREPARING THE EMMENTALER SPREAD

Place the cheese and cream in a bowl and stir until well blended.

ASSEMBLING AND BAKING THE CROQUE-MONSIEURS

Preheat the oven to 450°F (240°C/Gas Mark 8). Using a palette knife, spread an even layer of mustard butter over one side of each bread slice. Place butter side up on a baking sheet lined with parchment paper and toast in the oven for 5 minutes. Remove and reduce the oven temperature to 350°F (180°C/Gas Mark 4). Place a slice of ham on each slice of bread and top with Emmentaler spread. Bake for 15–20 minutes at 350°F (180°C/Gas Mark 4) until golden brown.

SURPRISE BREAD

Pain surprise

Makes 1 to serve 8–10

Active time
3 hours

***Pâte fermentée* fermentation time**
Overnight

Bulk fermentation time
30 minutes

Resting time
15 minutes

Proofing time
45 minutes–1 hour

Cooking time
40–50 minutes

Freezing time
30 minutes

Storage
Up to 24 hours

Equipment
Stand mixer + dough hook
Instant-read thermometer
6-in. (15-cm) cake ring, 8–10 in. (20–25 cm) deep
Bread lame
Serrated knife

Ingredients

Pâte fermentée
- ½ cup (2 oz./60 g) white bread flour (T65)
- 2 tbsp + 1¼ tsp (37 g/37 ml) water
- Scant ¼ tsp (1 g) salt
- 0.05 oz. (1 g) fresh yeast

Bread dough
- 2⅓ cups (9 oz./250 g) rye flour
- 2 cups (9 oz./250 g) white bread flour (T65)
- 2 tbsp (25 g) butter, diced, at room temperature
- 2 tsp (10 g) salt
- 0.5 oz. (15 g) fresh yeast
- 1½ cups (340 g/340 ml) water
- 3.5 oz. (100 g) *pâte fermentée* (see above)

Fillings
Different fillings of your choice, such as dried sausage, chorizo, ham, tapenade, cream cheese, etc.

PREPARING THE PÂTE FERMENTÉE (1 DAY AHEAD)
Mix the flour, water, salt, and yeast together in the bowl of the stand mixer and knead on low speed, or by hand, for 10 minutes until smooth. Place in a bowl, cover in plastic wrap, and let ferment overnight in the refrigerator.

PREPARING, SHAPING, AND PROOFING THE DOUGH
Knead all the dough ingredients in the bowl of the stand mixer on low speed for 4 minutes until well combined. Increase the speed to medium and knead for 6 minutes. Make sure the dough temperature does not exceed 75°F (24°C). Cover the bowl with plastic wrap and let ferment for 30 minutes at room temperature. Shape the dough into a ball and let rest for 15 minutes at room temperature. Place the cake ring on a baking sheet lined with parchment paper, and line the inside of the ring with parchment paper, too. Shape the dough into a tight ball (see technique p. 50) and place it in the ring. Dust the top of the dough evenly with flour and, using the bread lame, score it with a crosshatch cut (see technique p. 58). Let proof in a steam oven set to 75°F (24°C), or on a rack in a turned-off oven above a bowl of boiling water, for 45 minutes–1 hour.

BAKING THE BREAD
Place a rack in the center of the oven and another rack directly below it. Place a heavy-duty rimmed baking sheet on the bottom rack and preheat the oven to 450°F (240°C/Gas Mark 8). Bring 1 cup (250 ml) water to a simmer. Place the dough in the oven and carefully pour the simmering water into the rimmed sheet on the lower rack to create steam. Quickly close the oven door. Bake for 35–40 minutes, then carefully remove the ring and continue to bake for an additional 5–10 minutes until the sides are golden brown. Let the bread cool completely on a rack (see Chefs' Notes).

HOLLOWING OUT THE SURPRISE BREAD
Using the serrated knife, cut off the top of the loaf just beneath the scored part. To cut out the center of the bread, insert the knife vertically into the crumb, about ½ in. (1 cm) from the crust and until it reaches about ½ in. (1 cm) from the bottom of the loaf. Cut around the inside of the crust, leaving a ½-in. (1-cm) border all the way around. To release the crumb from the base, insert the knife into the side of the loaf with the blade parallel to the work surface, ½ in. (1 cm) from the bottom. Take care not to pierce the crust on the opposite side. Cut the crumb through this opening by carefully moving the blade forward, without moving the base of the knife (like a pivot). Remove the bread core and place it in the freezer for about 30 minutes to make it easier to slice. Cut the core crosswise into thin disks, about ¼ in. (5 mm) thick. Top half the disks with fillings of your choice and place one of the remaining disks on top of each one to make a sandwich. Cut each sandwich into 8–10 equal triangles and arrange in the hollowed-out base to refill it. Cover with the scored loaf top.

CHEFS' NOTES

Plan to bake the surprise bread one day ahead to make it easier to cut the next day.

HOT DOGS

Makes 8

Active time

1½ hours

Bulk fermentation time

15 minutes

Resting time

15 minutes

Proofing time

1–1¼ hours

Cooking time

15–20 minutes + poaching the pretzels and sausages

Storage

Unfilled pretzel buns: up to 24 hours

Equipment

Stand mixer + dough hook

Instant-read thermometer

Bread lame

Ingredients

Pretzel bun dough

4 cups + 2 tbsp (1 lb. 2 oz./500 g) white bread flour (T65)

1 cup (250 g/250 ml) whole milk

1¾ tsp (9 g) salt

5 tbsp (3 oz. /80 g) butter, diced, at room temperature

0.75 oz. (20 g) fresh yeast

2½ tsp (10 g) superfine sugar

5.25 oz. (150 g) ripe liquid levain (see technique p. 40)

4½ tsp (20 g/22 ml) sunflower oil

Poaching liquid

4 cups (1 kg/1 liter) water

¼ cup (1.75 oz./55 g) baking soda

Egg wash

1 egg white

Filling

8 Frankfurter sausages

8 tsp mustard

8 tsp ketchup

8 tbsp fried onions

PREPARING THE DOUGH

Knead all the pretzel dough ingredients in the bowl of the stand mixer on low speed for 3 minutes until well combined. Increase the speed to medium and knead for 10 minutes until the dough is supple and elastic. Make sure the dough temperature does not exceed 75°F (24°C). Place in a clean bowl, cover with plastic wrap, and let ferment for 15 minutes at room temperature. Divide the dough into 8 pieces weighing 3.75 oz. (105 g) each and shape each one into a ball. Let rest for 15 minutes at room temperature.

SHAPING AND PROOFING THE DOUGH

Shape each piece of dough into a mini-baguette shape (see technique p. 51), 6 in. (15 cm) long, and place on a baking sheet lined with parchment paper. Let proof in a steam oven set to 75°F (24°C), or on a rack in a turned-off oven above a bowl of boiling water, for 15–30 minutes, followed by 45 minutes in the refrigerator.

COOKING THE BUNS

Preheat the oven to 425°F (220°C/Gas Mark 7). Prepare the poaching liquid by combining the water and baking soda in a large saucepan. Bring to a boil and maintain at a simmer over low heat. Poach the pretzel buns in the simmering water for about 30 seconds on each side. Remove with a slotted spoon and return them to the parchment-lined baking sheet. Lightly whisk the egg white and brush over the buns. Using the bread lame, score the tops with diagonal slashes (see technique p. 57) or lengthwise down the center. Bake for 15–20 minutes. Let cool completely on a rack before filling.

PREPARING THE HOT DOGS

Poach the sausages for 10 minutes in a saucepan of simmering water. Preheat the broiler. Using the bread lame, cut the buns lengthwise down the center, without cutting all the way through, and spread the cut sides with mustard. Place the sausages in the buns and set on a baking sheet. Place under the broiler for a few minutes. Drizzle with ketchup, sprinkle with fried onions, and serve immediately.

HAM CROISSANTS

Croissant au jambon

Makes 8

Active time

2 hours

Cooking time

15 minutes + baking the croissants

Storage

Unfilled croissants: up to 24 hours

Equipment

Large serrated knife

Pastry bag with a plain round tip

Ingredients

Garlic-herb croissants

Base dough

1 cup (4.25 oz./125 g) all-purpose flour (*gruau*)

1 cup (4.25 oz./125 g) strong white bread flour (T65)

Generous 1/2 cup (135 g/135 ml) water at 39°F (4°C)

1 tbsp (15 g) milk powder

2 1/2 tbsp (1 oz./30 g) sugar

2 tsp (10 g) butter

0.5 oz. (12 g) fresh yeast

1 tsp (5 g) salt

1 1/4 tsp (5 g) garlic powder

3 1/2 tsp (5 g) herbes de Provence

Laminating butter

1 stick + 2 tbsp (5.25 oz./150 g) butter, preferably 84% butterfat

Béchamel

3 tbsp (1.75 oz./50 g) butter

Scant 1/2 cup (1.75 oz./50 g) flour

2 cups (500 g/500 ml milk

Salt, pepper, and a pinch of grated nutmeg

Fillings

8 slices ham (*jambon blanc*)

Grated Emmentaler cheese

PREPARING THE GARLIC-HERB CROISSANTS

Using the ingredients listed, prepare the yeasted pastry dough (see technique p. 74), incorporating the garlic powder and herbes de Provence in the second kneading stage (step 2 p. 74). Make 8 croissants with the dough and bake them (see technique p. 77). Let them cool completely before proceeding.

ASSEMBLING AND BAKING THE HAM CROISSANTS

Prepare the béchamel using the ingredients listed (see technique p. 122) and let cool. Preheat the oven to 350°F (180°C/Gas Mark 4). Using the serrated knife, cut the croissants in half horizontally. Spoon the béchamel into the pastry bag and pipe a layer over the bottom half of each croissant. Top with a slice of ham, then pipe out another layer of béchamel over the ham. Place the tops on the croissants. Place the croissants on a baking sheet lined with parchment paper, then pipe a little béchamel over the tops. Sprinkle with Emmentaler cheese. Bake for 15 minutes and serve immediately.

APPENDIXES

INDEX

INDEX (continued)

Acknowledgments

We would like to thank
Marine Mora and the **Matfer Bourgeat Group**
as well as the **Mora** store for the utensils and equipment.
www.matferbourgeat.com
www.mora.fr